PACIFIC MARINE FISHES

WARREN BURGESS & DR. HERBERT R. AXELROD

1. *Mirolabrichthys tuka* Herre. Purple queen. Photo of a five-inch specimen from Guadalcanal, Br. Solomon Islands, by Dr. Gerald R. Allen.

Book 6

FISHES OF MELANESIA

t.f.h.

ISBN 0-87666-128-2

Distributed in the U.S.A. by T.F.H. Publications, Inc., 211 West Sylvania Avenue, P.O. Box 27, Neptune City, N.J. 07753; in England by T.F.H. (Gt. Britain) Ltd., 13 Nutley Lane, Reigate, Surrey; in Canada to the book store and library trade by Clarke, Irwin & Company, Clarwin House, 791 St. Clair Avenue West, Toronto 10, Ontario; in Canada to the pet trade by Rolf C. Hagen Ltd., 3225 Sartelon Street, Montreal 382, Quebec; in Southeast Asia by Y.W. Ong, 9 Lorong 36 Geylang, Singapore 14; in Australia and the south Pacific by Pet Imports Pty. Ltd., P.O. Box 149, Brookvale 2100, N.S.W., Australia. Published by T.F.H. Publications Inc. Ltd., The British Crown Colony of Hong Kong.

TABLE OF CONTENTS

1. Family DASYATIDAE (*Stingrays*) 1393
2. Family ORECTOLOBIDAE
   (*Wobbegongs and Catsharks*) 1399
3. Family CONGRIDAE (*Conger Eels*) 1399
4. Family MURAENIDAE (*Moray Eels*) 1403
5. Family MORINGUIDAE (*Spaghetti or Thrush Eels*) 1410
6. Family ANOMALOPIDAE (*Lantern-eyes*) 1411
7. Family ATHERINIDAE (*Silversides or Hardyheads*) . . . 1412
8. Family SYNGNATHIDAE (*Pipefishes and Seahorses*) . . 1420
9. Family APOGONIDAE (*Cardinalfishes*) 1432
10. Family MULLIDAE (*Goatfishes*) 1461
11. Family NEMIPTERIDAE (*Butterfly-bream*) 1493
12. Family POMADASYIDAE (*Grunts, Sweetlips, etc.*) 1507
13. Family CHAETODONTIDAE (*Butterflyfishes*) 1520
14. Family POMACENTRIDAE
    (*Anemonefishes and Damselfishes*) 1545
15. Family BLENNIIDAE (*Blennies*) 1591
16. Family ACANTHURIDAE (*Surgeonfishes*) 1607

Covers:

Front Cover: *Manta birostris*. Photo by Pierre Laboute.
Anthias pleurotaenia. Photo by Dr. Gerald R. Allen.

Back Cover: *Mulloidichthys auriflamma*. Photo by Allan Power.
Amphiprion perideraion. Photo by Allan Power.

FISHES OF MELANESIA

INTRODUCTION

In the southwestern part of the Pacific Ocean there is a group of islands collectively called Melanesia. Included are such well-known islands or island groups as the Fiji Islands, Solomon Islands, New Hebrides, and Bismarck Archipelago, and such lesser known islands as the Santa Cruz and Loyalty Islands, although this last group includes New Caledonia, which should be recognizable separately. Also included as part of Melanesia is New Guinea, the largest island in the southwest Pacific (excluding the island continent of Australia). The islands of Melanesia spread over a vast area from New Guinea in the northwest to the Fiji Islands in the southeast. They are bordered on the west by the East Indies, on the north and northeast by Micronesia, on the east by Polynesia, on the southwest by Australia, and on the south by the cooler waters of the South Pacific. On one side of this island chain is the Pacific Ocean and on the other the Coral Sea. The Solomon Sea is included.

The fish fauna is therefore a mixture of elements from all these surrounding areas plus species which are found only in Melanesia or parts of it. Although many collections of fishes have been made in Melanesia, the fish fauna is still not that well known. It is hoped that the photos presented in this book will help make the fishes better known and bring to ichthyologists and aquarists some of their first glimpses of these fishes in their natural colors.

The islands covered in this book offer a tremendous variety of different habitats, just about every type that could be found in tropical regions. There are reef flats where one can walk across the tops of the corals at low tides and collect or view fishes and invertebrates without much equipment. There are shallow reefy areas where a swimmer can poke around corals and rocks in search of biological prizes. And of course there are the deeper reefs where more accomplished divers can collect or photograph the species unknown to the shallow waters and therefore not seen as often. For adventurous expert divers there are dropoffs to very deep water where the limits of SCUBA gear and physical prowess of the diver are the only barriers to the greater depths. Not every fish lives on the coral reefs, as you know, and there are sandy, rocky, and muddy areas where different types of fishes live. There are even variations in salinity for fishes that are able to venture into brackish or fresh waters.

As in earlier books of this series, we are again attempting to show the species of fishes two ways. First we give a fish 'portrait,' a photo which shows the fish close-up for identification purposes. Second, a photo or photos of the same species in its natural habitat gives the reader an idea of what it looks like in the wild. The portrait-type photos were taken by using a photo tank. The fish was placed in this small glass or plastic tank and further confined by use of a sheet of glass. The *in situ* photographs were taken through use of underwater cameras and aqualungs. Since the warm end of the light spectrum (reds and yellows) is filtered out quickly in depth so that the scene ultimately appears basically green or blue, an underwater flash is used to help render the colors more naturally. SCUBA gear is necessary for underwater fish photography. Fishes are much more easily approached by a slow moving diver, deeper water fishes can be photographed, and there is more time for the photographer to get that good pose that really shows the fish off to best advantage.

As we have done before, we try and represent the different aspects of the various fishes, presenting males and females if they look quite different, and juveniles if they too diverge from the typical adult patterns.

Some of the fishes in this book are species new to science and therefore specific names cannot be given. In future editions it is hoped that once the scientific descriptions have appeared we can rectify this situation. The new names will be incorporated into the cumulative indexes of future books as they become available.

The next book in this series will cover the greatest stretch of coral reef in the world, the Great Barrier Reef of Australia.

PACIFIC OCEAN
M E L A N E S I A
Admiralty Islands
BISMARCK SEA
Bismarck Archipelago
NEW GUINEA
SOLOMON SEA
British Solomon Islands
Guadalcanal
Santa Cruz Islands
Espíritu Santo Island
New Hebrides
New Caledonia
Loyalty Is.
Fiji
CORAL SEA
AUSTRALIA
0°
10°
20°
160°
170°E.
180°

2. One of the authors (HRA) hard at work photographing a clownfish, *Premnas biaculeatus*, using a photo tank. Photo by Heiko Bleher.

3. Underwater photographs are best taken while SCUBA diving. Photo of Dr. Herbert R. Axelrod by Heiko Bleher.

4. A view from the air of shallow reefs. Florida Island in the Br. Solomon Islands. Photo by Dr. Gerald R. Allen.

5. A stand of *Acropora* coral provides shelter for many different types of fishes. Lagoon reef at Malaita, Br. Solomon Islands. Photo by Dr. Gerald R. Allen.

6. Even shallow waters contain much that would interest collectors: corals, shells, other invertebrates, and small fishes. Photo by Dr. Herbert R. Axelrod in Fiji.

7. On the outer reef there may be a sheer drop-off to relatively deep water. Photo by Dr. Gerald R. Allen. Florida Island, Br. Solomon Islands.

8. *Taeniura lymma* (Forskal). The opening behind and below the eye is called the spiracle. Photo by Allan Power. New Hebrides.

9. *Taeniura lymma* (Forskal). Flashes or flood lights are necessary to bring out the true colors of an object underwater. Note how quickly the light fades out with distance. Photo by Dr. Herbert R. Axelrod. Marau, Br. Solomon Islands.

Family DASYATIDAE
STINGRAYS

One of the more colorful rays is *Taeniura lymma* with its tan disc liberally covered with bright blue spots. A bluish stripe is said to extend along each side of the tail from the back to behind the spines. It is a wide ranging species found throughout the tropical Indo-Pacific region and is fairly common in our area, where it frequents sandy lagoons among the coral formations. The food of the blue-spotted lagoon ray (also known as the lesser fantail ray) seems to consist of various invertebrates such as crustaceans (shrimps, stomatopods, etc.) and worms.

10. *Taeniura lymma* (Forskal). The same individual as above, but taken with the camera next to the light. Photo by Dr. Herbert R. Axelrod. Marau, Br. Solomon Islands.

11. *Amphotistius kuhli* (Muller and Henle). The spine on the tail can inflict painful wounds. Be careful when handling these stingrays. Photo by Dr. Herbert R. Axelrod. Marau, Br. Solomon Islands.

12. *Amphotistius kuhli* (Muller and Henle). Characteristic of this species are the blue-white spots on the disc and the black and white banded tail. Photo by Heiko Bleher. Marau, Br. Solomon Islands.

13. *Amphotistius kuhli* (Muller and Henle). Rays often lie buried in the sand with only the eyes and tail exposed. Photo by Heiko Bleher. Marau, Br. Solomon Islands.

14. *Amphotistius kuhli* (Muller and Henle). Found in shallows around coral reefs. Also referred to as *Dasyatis kuhli*. Photo by Allan Power. New Hebrides.

15. *Trygonorrhina fasciata* Muller and Henle. Fiddler ray. An easily identifiable ray more commonly found in Australia. Photo by Allan Power. New Hebrides.

16. *Manta birostris* (Walbaum). Although ominous in appearance, the devil rays are not dangerous. A school of goatfish is seen in the foreground. Photo by Pierre Laboute. New Caledonia.

17. *Stegostoma fasciatum* (Hermann). Adults of this species bear a striking superficial resemblance to the whale shark, *Rhincodon typus*. A juvenile is shown in PMF book 4, p. 1084. Photo by Pierre Laboute. New Caledonia.

Family ORECTOLOBIDAE
WOBBEGONGS AND CATSHARKS

Among the sharks most suitable for aquaria are the wobbegongs and catsharks. These are often attractively patterned with bold markings such as bands, splotches, stripes, and reticulations. The color patterns are such that they blend well with the background of their environment. Most species are bottom-dwelling sharks and some are dorso-ventrally flattened. They are generally found lying still on the bottom and have often been referred to as carpet sharks. It has been reported that bathers and waders may have provoked attacks by these sharks by inadvertently stepping on or near them. There are also reports of unprovoked attacks by these species.

The wobbegongs are usually classified in the genus *Orectolobus*. They are distinguishable from other orectolobids by the fringes or lobes found around the edge of the head, and the species may be distinguished by differences in the complexity of these fringes and the variety of color patterns. These bottom-living sharks are generally slow. Rather than actively pursue their prey, they lie in wait camouflaged by their color patterns. The tasseled fringes aid in this resemblance to the weed-covered bottoms they frequent. Wobbegongs are generally fairly large sharks ranging in size from six to twelve feet in length, with one poorly known species recorded as reaching only 1½ feet. In an aquarium the young of these sharks will do very well on a fish diet, although additions of some invertebrates such as octopuses and shellfish are recommended. The young are born alive.

Some of the smaller catsharks are included in the genus *Chiloscyllium* (PMF-4 pp. 1082-1083) and are well suited for home aquaria. These sharks normally reach only three or four feet in length and may be found in shallow waters around reefs or in bays. They do well if fed on fishes, squids, and various shellfish. Egg cases are occasionally found in weeds or washed up on shore, and if the embryo is still living and properly cared for, the aquarist might be treated with the sight of a shark hatching.

One of the more colorful of the orectolobids as a juvenile is *Stegostoma fasciatum* (PMF-4, p. 1084). Unfortunately it soon grows too large for most aquarists' tanks and reaches a full grown size of about eleven feet. It also outgrows its juvenile color pattern and becomes spotted as can be seen in the photo on p. 1398. In spite of its size this shark is generally considered harmless and feeds on molluscs and crustaceans, a diet that can probably be augmented with fish in the home aquarium. The leopard or zebra shark, as it is called, lays purplish-black egg cases a little over half a foot long and a few inches wide.

Family CONGRIDAE
CONGER EELS

For some fishes the best way to identify them to family is to eliminate all the other possible families first. These fishes are generally unspecialized and possess no particular characteristic that makes them stand out from the others. Conger eels fall into this category. Their lack of scales distinguishes them from the anguillids; they have superior or lateral nostrils in contrast to the ophichthiids where the posterior nostrils are labial; they generally do not have restricted gill openings like the muraenids (except in the specialized garden eels); and they do not have a projecting lower jaw (again the garden eels are exceptional in having an oblique mouth opening) like the anguillids or moringuids. In addition the gill openings are lateral as opposed to the ventrally located openings of the synaphobranchids, the tongue is free, and the teeth on the intermaxilla and vomer are not canine-like as compared with the muraenesocids which have an adnate tongue and canine teeth on the vomer and intermaxilla.

18. *Taenioconger hassi* Klausewitz. This garden eel has not been previously reported from the Pacific Ocean. It may, however, be subspecifically different from the Indian Ocean form. Photo by Dr. Herbert R. Axelrod. Marau, Br. Solomon Islands.

There are two major subfamilies: the Congrinae, with well developed pectoral fins and the body only moderately elongate; and the Heterocongrinae, commonly called garden eels, which have reduced or entirely absent pectoral fins and the body very elongate, the depth included 50 to 80 times in the length. Several conger eels are represented in PMF-2 p. 352.

Conger eels are cylindrical anteriorly but somewhat compressed posteriorly. They have well developed dorsal and anal fins but they are covered with thick skin. These fins are also confluent with the caudal fin. The anterior nostril is tubular and the posterior nostril is located at the level of the midpoint of the eye. The teeth are arranged in series and are present on the vomer and intermaxilla as well as in the jaws. They may be conical or flattened but not caniniform. The lips are thick and distinct.

Of the congrid eels, the species most likely to be found in the aquarium trade are the garden eels. These eels have attracted a great deal of attention by their habit

19. *Taenioconger hassi* Klausewitz. The color pattern is diagnostic. The anterior black spot marks the gill openings, the posterior one the anus. Photo by Dr. Herbert R. Axelrod. Marau, Br. Solomon Islands.

20. *Gorgasia maculata* Klausewitz. The head pores and lateral line pores are all encircled with white. This is one of the identifying characteristics of the species. Photo by Dr. Herbert R. Axelrod. Marau, Br. Solomon Islands.

21. *Gorgasia maculata* Klausewitz. Like other garden eels, the posterior end is usually in the burrow, with only the head and anterior part of the body sticking out. Photo by Dr. Herbert R. Axelrod. Marau, Br. Solomon Islands.

of hovering above their burrows in the sand, tail down, in large colonies or "gardens." The head of each individual is bent so that it is oriented toward the water currents and the body is relatively straight up-and-down. As divers approach a garden, these eels slowly and gradually sink back into their burrows so that when the diver is very near or actually over the burrow they are completely gone. As the diver continues on his way the eels farthest away will start to move back out of their burrow while those closest will still remain hidden. The gradation of amount of eel above the burrow from nearest to most distant is almost perfect. The garden eels hover over their burrow and pick small organisms from the water as they come drifting by.

If garden eels are to be kept in an aquarium they must be provided with a deep layer of fine sand for burrowing. This usually causes many problems for the aquarists, and such fishes are generally avoided. Some success has been achieved with burrowing fishes such as *Opisthognathus* species (jawfishes), and perhaps the same techniques can be applied to the garden eels. Being particulate plankton feeders, these eels most likely should be fed with small animals that can be kept in motion with the filter systems or air stones (live brine shrimp for example).

22. *Gymnothorax pictus* (Ahl). This species may also be called *Siderea picta*. Usually only 2½ feet in length. Photo by Allan Power. New Hebrides.

Family MURAENIDAE
MORAY EELS

The moray eels are one of the largest and most important groups of eels. They are quite familiar to almost every diver who swims about the reef and to many fishermen who have had the problem of whether or not to boat one of these creatures or simply to cut the line and be rid of it hook and all. Divers should be wary of poking around in holes in the reef since they might encounter one of these eels and irritate it enough so that it comes charging out of its hole on the attack. They have a wicked set of teeth, as can be seen in some of the accompanying photos, and have been known to inflict ugly wounds on the arms and legs of some people. Most morays, happily enough, will remain hidden in the protection of their holes if not disturbed. This 'shyness' makes it difficult to estimate the moray population of a reef, and only by a systematic poisoning of a section of the reef can an approximation of their number be established. And the number encountered is sure to astound the census taker.

Morays are rather robust eels, very strong, with some species reaching lengths of six feet or more. Most morays are smaller, attaining sizes of only about two to three feet. A moray eel's body is usually rounded to slightly compressed, scaleless, and covered with a tough skin which extends over the dorsal and anal fins. These fins are well developed or rudimentary and are confluent with the caudal fin. The pectoral and pelvic fins are absent. The mouth cleft is wide and gaping, and the jaws will not close completely, giving these fishes a sinister look to go along with their bad reputation. The teeth are round, compressed, or conical, some of the anterior ones fang-like. These anterior teeth are depressable posteriorly, lying back as the prey is swallowed but becoming erect and preventing escape if the prey is able to reverse its direction. In one of the genera the teeth are modified into a pavement-like structure adept at crushing molluscs.

Morays can be tamed to some extent, and enterprising divers on some television programs have shown how they feed these eels by hand. This is quite spectacular treatment of one of the so-called denizens of the deep, but it is definitely not recommended, especially if you value your fingers.

23. Unidentified species of *Gymnothorax*. The rotation of the eyes allows for binocular vision to some extent in these eels. Photo by Dr. Herbert R. Axelrod. Marau, Br. Solomon Islands.

Most of the moray eels collected for home aquaria belong to three genera, *Gymnothorax*, *Echidna*, and *Rhinomuraena*. The last-mentioned genus includes the well-known black and blue ribbon eels that have gained so much popularity in the aquarium trade. The species of *Echidna* are usually strikingly patterned, such as the zebra moray (*E. zebra*) and the starry moray (*E. nebulosa*), and are the mollusc-

24. *Gymnothorax zonipectus* Seale. The white markings about the head help to identify this species. A dark spot is also normally present behind each eye. Photo by Dr. Herbert R. Axelrod. Marau, Br. Solomon Islands.

crushers. The largest, *Gymnothorax*, contains practically all of the other moray eels that you may find in the aquarium trade. Some species are very colorful and make bright additions to a marine tank.

Identification of moray eels is very difficult, the major distinguishing characteristics being number and placement of the teeth and the color pattern (which is highly variable). Feeding moray eels is relatively easy. Although by far the preference is for squids and octopuses, they will generally do well on pieces of fish, molluscs, and crustaceans. Any aquarium with moray eels should have plenty of hiding places (rocks, coral, etc.), a top or cover, and tankmates too large for it to swallow, or they will start disappearing overnight as the nocturnally hunting eel takes its toll.

25. *Gymnothorax zonipectus* Seale. This species is known from Java and the Philippines to Tahiti. Photo by Dr. Herbert R. Axelrod. Marau, Br. Solomon Islands.

26. An unidentified species of *Gymnothorax*. Moray eels can be dangerous. A look at these teeth should be sufficient warning to anybody to be careful. Photo by Allan Power. New Hebrides.

27. *Gymnothorax* sp. (possibly *G. thyrsoidea*). Small moray eels are occasionally offered for sale in aquarium shops. They make a very good 'conversation piece.' Photo by Dr. Herbert R. Axelrod. Marau, Br. Solomon Islands.

28. *Gymnothorax* sp. (possibly *G. thyrsoidea*). The anterior nostrils of morays are tubular as shown in this photo. Photo by Dr. Herbert R. Axelrod. Marau, Br. Solomon Islands.

29. ?*Gymnothorax undulatus* (Lacepede). This species grows to a length of about 6 feet. Photo by Dr. Herbert R. Axelrod. Marau, Br. Solomon Islands.

30. ?*Gymnothorax undulatus* (Lacepede). This specimen is small and the identification is tentative. Photo by Dr. Herbert R. Axelrod. Marau, Br. Solomon Islands.

31. *Gymnothorax flavimarginatus* (Ruppell). Note the black spot marking the position of the gill opening. Photo by Dr. Herbert R. Axelrod. Marau, Br. Solomon Islands.

32. *Gymnothorax meleagris* (Shaw). A widely distributed species, occurring throughout much of the Indo-Pacific region. Photo by Allan Power. New Hebrides.

33. ?*Moringua microchir* Bleeker. The eyes in the thrush eels are small or, as in this case, nearly hidden below the skin. Photo by Dr. Herbert R. Axelrod. Marau, Br. Solomon Islands.

34. *Rhinomuraena quaesita* Garman. This ribbon eel was estimated to be about 20" in length. Photo by Dr. Gerald R. Allen. Rabaul, New Britain in 15' of water.

Family MORINGUIDAE
SPAGHETTI OR THRUSH EELS

Moringuids are long, slender eels resembling somewhat an elongate worm or a string of spaghetti, as the common name implies. They may be found in a variety of shallow inshore habitats, wherever there is a suitable substrate for burrowing, in marine or brackish waters. They are excellent burrowers and can travel quite rapidly through loose sand just below the surface. In contrast to most other burrowing eels, which are notably tail-first burrowers, the moringuids dive head first into the sand, mud, or gravel.

There presently is no satisfactory combination of characteristics which will define these eels, particularly because of the radical changes which occur as the eel grows into adulthood. Additionally, there is sexual dimorphism, the extent of which is still undetermined in some forms. The young or immature eels, like the one pictured here, are said to have reduced eyes (in this case they are small and covered with a membrane), probably as an adaptation to the burrowing existence. Their fins are reduced, the small pectoral is placed very low, and the dorsal and anal fins are low and located posteriorly on the tail section. A caudal fin is present. As these eels mature the pectoral fin develops and the dorsal and anal fins become higher. The caudal fin may develop lobes. The eyes become larger and the skin or membrane covering them disappears. One interesting feature of these eels is that the heart is located far behind the gills. In contrast to the worm eels (Ophichthidae) which have the anterior nostrils tubular and located on the edge of the upper lip or the ventral surface of the snout, the spaghetti eels have them laterally or even superiorly.

The adults continue the burrowing habit of the young, but with the development of the fins and eyes they often appear in open water at night. They are caught while night-lighting but evidently remain beneath the sand during the day.

Although unique and interesting eels they would not normally be kept in marine aquaria.

35. ?*Moringua microchir* Bleeker. The worm-like structure is often encountered in burrowing eels. Photo by Dr. Herbert R. Axelrod. Marau, Br. Solomon Islands.

Family ANOMALOPIDAE
LANTERN-EYES

Living light or, to use the more scientific term, bioluminescence can be found in several types of animals including fishes. In fishes bioluminescence can usually be divided into two categories, luminescence that arises from photophores (light organs composed of cells arranged to form glands) which are under the control of endocrine glands, and luminescence that is the result of accumulations of light-producing bacteria living in a symbiotic relationship with the fish. These bacteria are confined to specific areas, usually with associated structures to govern the amount of light emitted. In the family Anomalopidae the fishes have a bar composed of a series of tubes which house the luminescent bacteria beneath each eye. Since the bacteria are not under endocrine control by the fish, the light must be regulated by mechanical means. This is usually accomplished by two methods in this family. First, the windowshade method, which is simply a dark eyelid which can be pulled up over the light organ, obscuring the light from the bacteria. Secondly, a muscular attachment rotates the organ so that the light is directed into the fish and is no longer visible from the outside. The first method is found in genus *Photoblepharon*, the second in *Anomalops.*

Photoblepharon palpebratus is a small fish, of about 3½ inches, with a single dorsal fin. It can maintain the light for almost 30 minutes, after which it becomes more erratic.

Anomalops katoptron is larger, reaching about a foot in length, has two dorsal fins, and the light is emitted for at most 10 seconds at a time. It is nocturnal, hiding during the day and coming out at night (especially moonless nights), when their blue-green lights can be seen pulsating every few seconds. At Marau Island and Lau Lasi Island (an artificial island) it lives in stone walls during the day but is collected for food by the local people at night when it comes out. The light organ can be rotated 180° with the axis of the body so that it is visible or not, and also rotated forward at an angle of 90° with the body for a more prominent display. These fishes do well in the aquarium if kept alone, though one should be resigned to seeing them only at night.

The third and only other known species in the family is a Caribbean species, *Kryptophanaron alfredi*. This fish was described by Fowler several decades ago from Jamaica and is very poorly known.

At least one species, *Anomalops katoptron*, is found in shallow water. It is one of the very few non-deep sea luminescent fishes, another common example being the midshipman (a toadfish) of the southern United States.

36. *Anomalops katoptron* (Bleeker). The light organ below the eye is very conspicuous but can be "turned off" by rotation of the organ. Photo by Dr. Herbert R. Axelrod. Marau, Br. Solomon Islands.

Family ATHERINIDAE
SILVERSIDES OR HARDYHEADS

Silversides are small fishes that are generally characterized by a silvery stripe along the side. They have two widely spaced dorsal fins in which the first is weak, prompting ichthyologists to place them near the barracudas and mullets, which have a similar dorsal fin arrangement. Recent findings, however, have now caused the shuffling of some of these fishes around and the silversides and related families (Melanotaeniidae, Phallostethidae, etc.) which make up the suborder Atherinoidei, are considered more closely related to the members of the suborder Cyprinodontoidei (killifishes, livebearers, etc.).

Silversides generally occur in large schools along the shore and may be found in marine, brackish or fresh water, though the majority are marine. The large schools of small silversides are constantly preyed upon by larger fishes. They themselves are carnivorous, feeding mostly on zooplankton. As might be expected with this type of feeding, the gill rakers are numerous and the mouth large but with small teeth.

Spawning occurs in the shallows where large greenish eggs are laid. These eggs are provided with long, sticky filaments like those of the flyingfishes (which are included in the same order Atheriniformes), and which become entwined in the sea grasses or other aquatic plants of the bottom, anchoring them there until they hatch. There are exceptions to this method of spawning within the family, the best-known of which is the California grunion. The grunion move onto the beaches of California at night at peak high tides. The female partially burrows into the wet sand and the male wraps himself around her, fertilizing the eggs as they are laid. The eggs remain buried about two inches deep in the sand until the time of the next highest tides, when they hatch as the water washes over them.

Silversides are not usually considered aquarium fishes and at most may be used as food for some of the larger fishes such as groupers or scorpionfishes. The melanotaenids, which are sometimes included in this family, on the other hand are well-known fresh water aquarium favorites (Australian rainbowfish, etc.).

37. ?*Pranesus pinguis* (Lacepede). Schools of this silverside can be seen around harbors and bays. Photo by Dr. Herbert R. Axelrod. Marau, Br. Solomon Islands.

38. Unidentified clupeid, probably a *Sardinella* or *Harengula*. Schooling fishes like these form one of the food sources for the reef predators. Photo by Allan Power. New Hebrides.

39. *Sphyraena* sp. Young barracuda often hunt in these "wolf packs" but become more solitary predators as they grow older. Photo by Allan Power, New Hebrides.

40. *Hemirhamphus commersoni* Cuvier. The barred halfbeak schools in bays and harbors. It is often found around weedy areas. Photo by Dr. Herbert R. Axelrod. Marau, Br. Solomon Islands.

41. *Hemirhamphus commersoni* Cuvier. The eyes face partially downward in this surface living fish, presumably to spot predators coming from below. Photo by Dr. Herbert R. Axelrod. Marau, Br. Solomon Islands.

42. *Aeoliscus strigatus* (Gunther). It is advisable to place more than one of these fishes in an aquarium. A solitary individual usually doesn't do as well as when it has company. Photo by Dr. Herbert R. Axelrod. Marau, Br. Solomon Islands.

43. *Aeoliscus strigatus* (Gunther). Shrimpfish may use the protection afforded by coral branches. Note the thinness of one fish turned belly to the observer (second from left). Photo by Michio Goto from the book *Marine Life Documents.*

44. *Aeoliscus strigatus* (Gunther). This photo taken in the field shows how the shrimpfish are protected by the spines of the long-spined black sea urchin. The black stripe on the fish may also be involved with this behavior. Photo by Pierre Laboute. New Caledonia.

45. ?*Pempheris vanicolensis* Cuvier. Barely visible are the dark markings on the dorsal, anal and caudal fins. Photo by Dr. Gerald R. Allen of a 6-inch specimen. Guadalcanal, Br. Solomon Islands at about 35' depth.

46. *Parapriacanthus dispar* (Herre). The more elongate body and the fewer anal fin rays indicate this is a member of the genus *Parapriacanthus* rather than *Pempheris*. Photo by Dr. Herbert R. Axelrod. Marau, Br. Solomon Islands.

47. A group of pempherids, probably also *Parapriacanthus dispar* (Herre), on the reef. Photo by Pierre Laboute. New Caledonia.

When presented with a choice of whether to bring home a seahorse or pipefish for his marine tank, an aquarist will almost always decide in favor of the seahorse. Its shape and habits make a seahorse an attention getter right from the start. They are not difficult to care for, and a good supply of live brine shrimp will often be sufficient.

Certain pipefishes are popular because of their attractive color pattern, the most notable of these being *Doryrhamphus melanopleura* and *Dunckerocampus dactyliophorus*. Actually there are two species of *Dunckerocampus* that might find their way to aquarists tanks, *D. dactyliophorus* and *D. caulleryi*. Both are banded and have the red and white (or yellowish) tail fin. The two species can easily be separated by noting the number of bands crossing the opercle: *D. caulleryi* has two crossing it, *D. dactyliophorus* has only one. Once the species has been correctly established the sexes can be told apart by the banding as well according to some workers in the group. Males generally have a greater number of red bands than do females. In *D. caulleryi* males have about 30-31 bands (total) and females have about 26 or 27; in *D. dactyliophorus* males may also have one or more bands more than females, but this has not been confirmed. If it is true the individual in PMF-2 (p. 235) would be a female and the one pictured here would be a male. Unfortunately they were not taken in the same area and the differences might be regarded as geographical variation.

Pipefishes, like the seahorses, do well on live brine shrimp or newly born guppies.

Dunckerocampus species have the brooding area on the abdomen, but the eggs are usually unsheltered by pouch folds or flaps. Other pipefishes might have eggs attached to the tail rings and in either position may have some sort of protective flaps or pouch. The pouch in pipefishes extends from the side to cover the eggs, the flaps meeting in the middle of the egg area. That in seahorses is always on the tail rings and sealed except for a small opening near the upper end.

48. Dunckerocampus dactyliophorus (Bleeker). The small mouth is well suited for selecting small animals as prey. Brine shrimp are an excellent food for seahorses and pipefishes. Photo by Dr. Herbert R. Axelrod. Marau, Br. Solomon Islands.

49. *Dunckerocampus dactyliophorus* (Bleeker). The eggs are attached to the abdomen of the male of this species where they remain until hatching. Unlike most seahorses or some other pipefishes, the eggs are not within a "pouch" but are relatively unprotected. Photo by Dr. Herbert R. Axelrod. Marau, Br. Solomon Islands.

50. *Parapercis tetracantha* (Lacepede). The dorsal fin spines are to be avoided as they can inflict painful wounds when handled. Photo by Dr. Gerald R. Allen of a 5-inch specimen from Madang, New Guinea (20 feet deep).

51. *Parapercis clathrata* Ogilby. Weevers are carnivorous and do well in aquaria. Small fishes are not recommended as tank mates. Photo by Dr. Gerald R. Allen of a 6-inch specimen in Madang, New Guinea (20 feet deep).

52. *Parapercis cylindrica* (Bloch). Notice the conspicuous white pelvic fins in this and other species of *Parapercis*. Photo by Pierre Laboute. New Caledonia.

53. *Aulostomus chinensis* (Linnaeus). Though long and slender, the trumpet fish has a fairly large mouth and cannot be trusted in an aquarium with smaller fishes. Photo by Allan Power. New Hebrides.

54. A lizardfish, probably *Synodus variegatus*, sitting in the branches of a soft coral. Photo by Dr. Herbert R. Axelrod. Marau, Br. Solomon Islands.

55. *Synodus variegatus* (Lacepede). The variegated lizardfish reaches a size of about 10 to 11 inches. This one, taken at a depth of about 30 feet, is about six inches long. Photo by Dr. Gerald R. Allen. Madang, New Guinea.

56. *Synodus variegatus* (Lacepede). The natural colors of this fish blend well with the background of the reef here. Photo of a six-inch specimen by Dr. Gerald R. Allen. Guadalcanal, Br. Solomon Islands (40 feet deep).

57. *Synodus variegatus* (Lacepede). Lizardfishes possess an adipose fin as can be seen in this photo. Photo by Dr. Herbert R. Axelrod. Marau, Br. Solomon Islands.

58. *Synodus variegatus* (Lacepede). Under proper lighting the true color of the eyes can be seen. In this photo they are reflecting blue. Photo by Allan Power. Santo, New Hebrides.

59. *Synodus variegatus* (Lacepede). Living up to its name, the variegated lizardfish has changed its pattern to a horizontal mid-lateral band. Photo by Allan Power. Santo, New Hebrides.

60. *Saurida gracilis* Quoy and Gaimard. The rows of cardiform teeth can easily be seen in this close up view of the slender saury. Photo by Dr. Herbert R. Axelrod. Marau, Br. Solomon Islands.

61. *Saurida gracilis* Quoy and Gaimard. This species can grow to a length of about one foot. Photo by Dr. Herbert R. Axelrod. Marau, Br. Solomon Islands.

62. *Synodus variegatus* (Lacepede). Another pattern in the repertoire of the variegated lizardfish. Photo by Dr. Herbert R. Axelrod. Marau, Br. Solomon Islands.

63. A group of young fishes, probably *Pholidichthys leucotaenia*, which bear a strong resemblance to the young plotosid catfishes. Photo by Heiko Bleher. Marau, Br. Solomon Islands.

64. *Plotosus anguillaris* (Bloch). Although pet shop specimens of plotosids are small, they grow to 3 feet in length in nature. Photo by Dr. Gerald R. Allen. Guadalcanal, Br. Solomon Islands (40 feet deep).

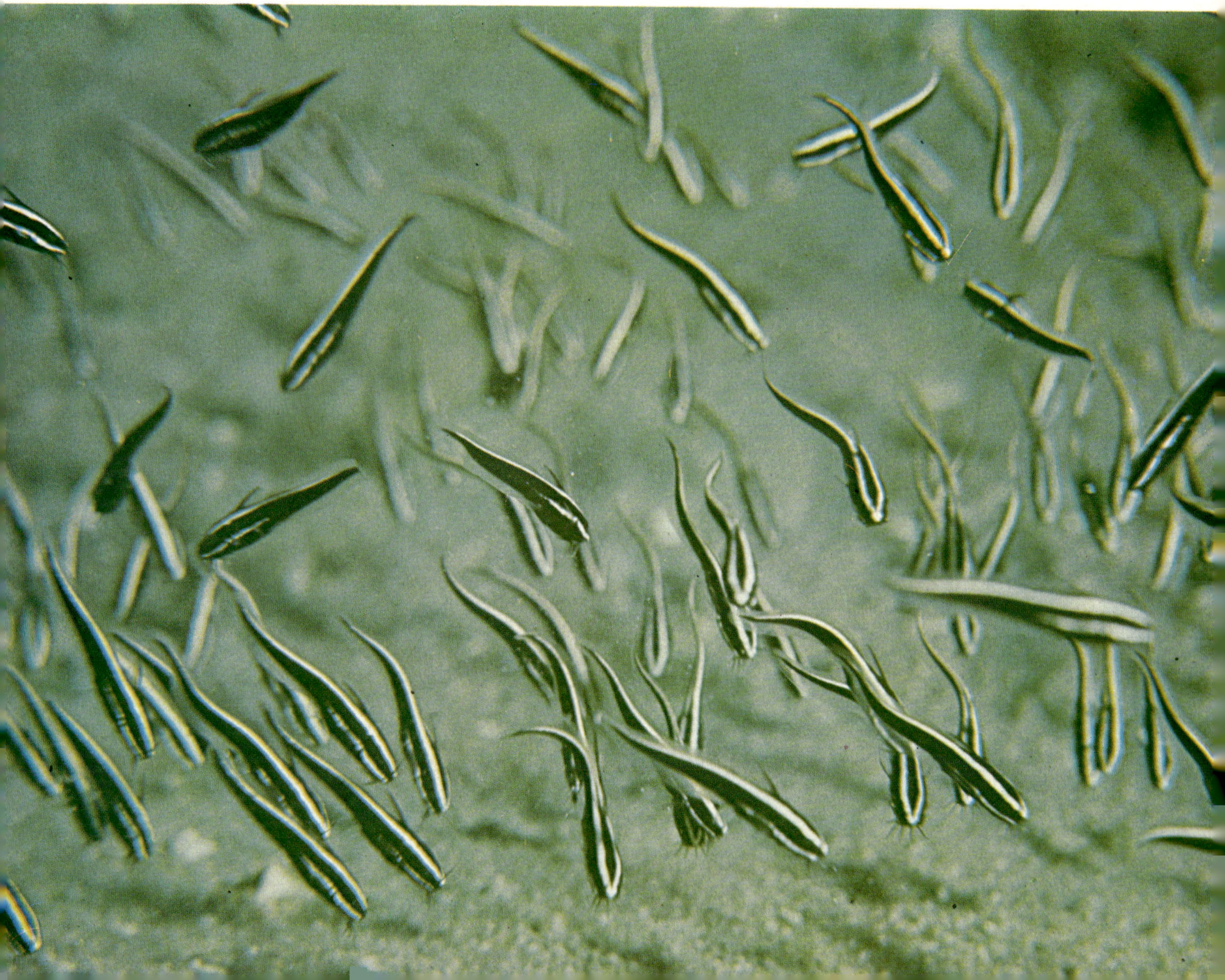

65. *Plotosus anguillaris* (Bloch). Plotosids occur in marine, brackish, and even fresh waters, sometimes ascending rivers. Note the non-plotosid fishes in the foreground of the photo. Photo by Pierre Laboute. New Caledonia.

66. A school of young glassfishes (family Centropomidae) looking very much like young cardinalfishes. Many fishes when young can be found in small schools even though they may be more solitary as they mature. Photo by Heiko Bleher. Marau, Br. Solomon Islands.

67. *Cheilodipterus* sp. Cardinalfishes are not usually seen out in the open like this except at night. Photo by Dr. Herbert R. Axelrod. Marau, Br. Solomon Islands.

68. *Apogon aroubiensis* Hombron and Jacquinot. Cardinalfishes can often be found under rocks, in caves, or under rock ledges such as this one. Photo by Dr. Herbert R. Axelrod. Marau, Br. Solomon Islands.

69. Pempherids, apogonids, and pomacentrids are all congregating in the protection of the spines of this long-spined black sea urchin. Photo by Pierre Laboute. New Caledonia.

Family APOGONIDAE
CARDINALFISHES

Aside from a few favorites, cardinalfishes are not prominent in marine aquaria. This is rather surprising since in the following pages a number of magnificent apogonids can be seen that would rival some of the more popular marine species currently kept. Some of these cardinalfishes are mouthbrooders (or oral incubators if you prefer that terminology), which would make them even more desirable. Perhaps their time will come.

Most of the cardinalfishes pictured here are included in genera that have been discussed before. Only one genus is new to this series of books, and that is *Pseudamia*. This small apogonid belongs to the group with some prominent canines, but can be distinguished from the other genera (*Cheilodipterus, Synagrops*, etc.,) by the absence of a complete lateral line.

We are happy to finally be able to present to you the two orbiculate cardinalfish species, *Sphaeramia orbicularis* and *S. nematoptera*, so that the differences can clearly be seen. The common aquarium apogonid is *S. nematoptera*, even though it has been sold under *S. orbicularis* on many occasions. In *S. orbicularis* the colors are not as gaudy and the black band is narrower; it also has orange spots in the dorsal fin and only the posterior portion of the pelvic fins blackish (both these fins in *S. nematoptera* are mostly dark brownish or blackish). Incidentally, both these species are said to be mouthbrooders, the male probably caring for the eggs. In some of the cardinals more than one hundred eggs are cared for at one time. Imagine the sight of one hundred baby cardinalfishes milling around the parent and then on signal all dashing into his mouth for protection.

70. *Cheilodipterus macrodon* (Lacepede). From the appearance of the branchial area, this cardinalfish could be incubating eggs. Photo by Allan Power. Santo, New Hebrides.

71. *Cheilodipterus quinquelineatus* Cuvier or *C. isostigma* (Schultz). The only way to tell these two species apart is by dentition. Photo by Dr. Herbert R. Axelrod. Marau, Br. Solomon Islands.

72. *Cheilodipterus macrodon* (Lacepede). This species gets rather large in nature, about 8 inches, but normally does not exceed five to six inches in an aquarium. Photo by Allan Power. Santo, New Hebrides.

73. Two species of cardinalfishes are sharing the sea urchins. The yellow-striped one is probably *Apogon cyanosoma*, the dark-striped one probably *A. compressus*. Photo by Allan Power. Santo, New Hebrides.

74. *Apogon cyanosoma* Bleeker. This species may also be called *Gronovichthys cyanosoma*. Photo by Dr. Herbert R. Axelrod. Marau, Br. Solomon Islands.

75. *Apogon cyanosoma* Bleeker. The incomplete yellow stripe on the body may eventually fuse with the one below it. Photo by Dr. Gerald R. Allen of a 4-inch specimen. Guadalcanal, Br. Solomon Islands (30 feet deep).

76. *Apogon compressus* (Smith and Radcliffe). Called the split-band cardinalfish because of the bifurcate band just above and behind the eye. Photo of a 3-inch specimen by Dr. Gerald R. Allen. Madang, New Guinea (20 feet deep).

77. *Apogon aroubiensis* Hombron and Jacquinot. This species apparently occurs from the East Indies and the Philippines throughout most of Melanesia. Photo by Dr. Herbert R. Axelrod. Marau, Br. Solomon Islands.

78. *Apogon taeniophorus* Regan. The striped forms of cardinalfishes are very hard to tell apart This species is often synonymized with *A. novemfasciatus*. Photo by Dr. Herbert R. Axelrod. Marau, Br. Solomon Islands.

79. *Apogon aroubiensis* Hombron and Jacquinot. In this species the light stripes are much narrower than the dark ones. Photo by Dr. Gerald R. Allen of a 3-inch specimen from Guadalcanal, Br. Solomon Islands. (30 feet deep).

80. *Cheilodipterus zonatus* Smith and Radcliffe. With the first dorsal fin folded back this cardinalfish looks very streamlined. Photo of a 3½-inch specimen by Dr. Gerald R. Allen. Madang, New Guinea (10 feet deep).

81. *Apogon* sp. (possibly *A. hartzfeldi*). The pattern of a white line along the back is not often seen in these fishes. Photo by Aaron Norman.

82. *Apogon kallopterus* Bleeker. Many species of cardinalfishes incubate the eggs in their mouth. Photo by Dr. Herbert R. Axelrod. Marau, Br. Solomon Islands.

83. *Apogon kallopterus* Bleeker. It is difficult to determine the exact range of this species due to its confusion with other striped species. Photo by Dr. Herbert R. Axelrod. Marau, Br. Solomon Islands.

84. *Apogon kallopterus* Bleeker. Note the width of the lateral band as compared to *A. fraenatus* on the opposite page. Photo by Dr. Herbert R. Axelrod. Marau, Br. Solomon Islands.

85. *Apogon fraenatus* Valenciennes. The original specimens of this species were discovered at New Guinea and Guam. Photo by Dr. Herbert R. Axelrod. Marau, Br. Solomon Islands.

86. *Pseudamia gelatinosa* Smith. This species may eventually turn out to be the earlier described *P. polystigma*. Photo by Dr. Herbert R. Axelrod. Marau, Br. Solomon Islands.

87. *Apogon sealei* Fowler. This species is poorly known and may be restricted to Melanesia and the Philippine Islands. Photo by Dr. Gerald R. Allen of a 4-inch individual from Port Moresby, New Guinea (20 feet deep).

88. *Archamia* sp. This cardinalfish may be an undescribed species. Photo of two 3-inch individuals by Dr. Gerald R. Allen. Guadalcanal, Br. Solomon Islands (30' deep).

89. *Apogon* sp. This fish is under study as a possible new species. Photo by Dr. Herbert R. Axelrod. Marau, Br. Solomon Islands.

90. *Archamia leai* Waite. Many apogonids occur in groups such as this one. Perhaps it is best to keep several in an aquarium rather than one. Photo by Allan Power. Santo, New Hebrides.

91. *Archamia zosterophora* (Bleeker). This species is apparently known in the limited area from the East Indies and the Philippines to New Guinea. Photo of 3-inch individuals by Dr. Gerald R. Allen. Madang, New Guinea (25 feet deep).

92. *Apogon fragilis* Smith. This fish should not be confused with *Sceptarias fragilis* (= *Epigonus atherinoides*), which is a deep water cardinalfish from the Hawaiian Islands and Japan. Photo by Dr. Gerald R. Allen of 3-inch specimens. Madang, New Guinea (6 feet deep).

93. *Gymnapogon urospilotus* Lachner. The dark marking at the base of the caudal fin is distinctive. Photo by Dr. Herbert R. Axelrod. Marau, Br. Solomon Islands.

94. *Apogon leptacanthus* Bleeker. This beautiful species would certainly be welcomed as an aquarium fish. Photo of 3-inch long specimens by Dr. Gerald R. Allen. Madang, New Guinea.

95. *Archamia fucata* (Cantor). The electric blue lines around the snout are well represented in this photo. Photo by Allan Power. Santo, New Hebrides.

96. *Archamia biguttata* Lachner. The anterior black spot makes this species readily recognizable. Photo of a 3-inch specimen by Dr. Gerald R. Allen. Guadalcanal, Br. Solomon Islands. (35 feet deep).

97. *Archamia fucata* (Cantor). This species is very closely related to *A. lineolata.* Photo by Dr. Herbert R. Axelrod. Marau, Br. Solomon Islands.

98. *Archamia fucata* (Cantor). This species is usually seen in small groups. Photo by Dr. Herbert R. Axelrod. Marau, Br. Solomon Islands.

99. *Apogon savayensis* Gunther. The eye may be showing the effects of decompression from deep water. Photo by Dr. Herbert R. Axelrod. Marau, Br. Solomon Islands.

100. *Archamia fucata* (Cantor). With proper lighting the silvery background accents the orange lines of the body. Photo by Dr. Gerald R. Allen of a 4-inch individual.

101. *Apogon aureus* (Lacepede). The ring-tailed càrdinalfish may also be known under the name *Gronovichthys aureus*. Photo by Allan Power. Santo, New Hebrides.

102. *Sphaeramia orbicularis* (Cuvier). This is the real *S. orbicularis* and should be compared with *S. nematoptera* below. Photo of a 3-inch individual by Dr. Gerald R. Allen. Madang, New Guinea (3 feet deep).

103. *Sphaeramia nematoptera* (Bleeker). This is the well known aquarium species. It does very well in captivity. Photo by Dr. Gerald R. Allen. Madang, New Guinea (20 feet deep).

104. *Myripristis violaceus* Bleeker. This seven-inch individual was photographed at a depth of 30 feet. Photo by Dr. Gerald R. Allen. Florida Island, Br. Solomon Islands.

105. *Myripristis vittatus* Cuvier and Valenciennes. The lack of black or dusky color around the operculum and pectoral fin base is unusual in this genus. Photo by Dr. Gerald R. Allen of a 6-inch specimen from Florida Island, Br. Solomon Islands (20 feet deep).

106. *Myripristis pralinus* Cuvier. One report states that on death golden longitudinal bands appear along the scale rows. Photo by Dr. Herbert R. Axelrod. Marau, Br. Solomon Islands.

107. *Myripristis violaceus* Bleeker. Do not confuse this species of soldierfish with the squirrelfish *Adioryx violaceus*. Photo by Dr. Herbert R. Axelrod. Marau, Br. Solomon Islands.

108. *Myripristis murdjan* (Forskal). Soldierfishes often occur in small groups in caves or under ledges. These are about 6 inches in length. Photo by Dr. Gerald R. Allen. Florida Island, Br. Solomon Islands (20 feet deep).

109. *Adioryx caudimaculatus* (Ruppell). The identifying white spot on the caudal peduncle is lost in the whiteness of the posterior end of this individual. Photo by Allan Power. Santo, New Hebrides.

110. *Flammeo sammara* (Forskal). The slender red stripes on the body and the dark spot in the dorsal fin are characteristic of this species. Photo by Dr. Herbert R. Axelrod. Marau, Br. Solomon Islands.

111. *Adioryx diadema* (Lacépede). Here the broad stripes are red and the narrow ones light. The dorsal fin pattern is also of value in identifying this species. Photo by Dr. Herbert R. Axelrod. Marau, Br. Solomon Islands.

112. *Flammeo operculare* (Valenciennes). The solid dark band in the dorsal fin and the yellow in the tail fin help identify the black-finned squirrel-fish. Photo by Dr. Herbert R. Axelrod. Marau, Br. Solomon Islands.

113. *Flammeo operculare* (Valenciennes). This wary squirrelfish is probably ready to flee into the dark cave in the background as the photographer approaches. Photo by Allan Power. Santo, New Hebrides.

114. *Adioryx violaceus* (Bleeker). A full grown individual of this species will reach a size of about 9 inches. Photo by Dr. Herbert R. Axelrod. Marau, Br. Solomon Islands.

115. *Adioryx violaceus* (Bleeker). For a diagnostic photo a specimen is pinned out in a wax tray and treated with formalin. Photo by Dr. Herbert R. Axelrod. Marau, Br. Solomon Islands.

116. *Adioryx spinifer* (Forskal). Once the pins are removed the fins will stay spread if the proper procedure was followed. Spread fins make counts and identification much easier. Photo by Dr. Herbert R. Axelrod. Marau, Br. Solomon Islands.

117. *Adioryx violaceus* (Bleeker). The red color of this fish does not stand out as greatly when other red objects are close by. Photo by Allan Power. Santo, New Hebrides.

118. *Adioryx spinifer* (Forskal). Normally the bright red or vermillion dorsal fin is folded back, as in this photo. Photo by Allan Power. Santo, New Hebrides.

119. *Adioryx cornutum* (Bleeker). The three blackish spots at the bases of the soft dorsal, anal, and caudal fins are characteristic. Photo by Dr. Herbert R. Axelrod. Marau, Br. Solomon Islands.

120. *Adioryx cornutum* (Bleeker). Few predators could follow this squirrelfish into the sharp coral behind it. Photo by Dr. Gerald R. Allen. Madang, New Guinea (20 feet deep).

121. *Adioryx tieroides* (Bleeker). One of the lesser known squirrelfishes, this species reaches about 7 inches in length. Photo by Dr. Herbert R. Axelrod. Marau, Br. Solomon Islands.

122. *Adioryx caudimaculatus* (Ruppell). Note the color change between this fish and the one on p. 1451. Photo by Dr. Herbert R. Axelrod. Marau, Br. Solomon Islands.

123. *Priacanthus* sp. This young bigeye (Priacanthidae) has its mouth fully extended. When considering them for aquarium fishes this mouth capacity must be taken into account. Photo by Dr. Herbert R. Axelrod. Marau, Br. Solomon Islands.

124. *Trachinotus blochii* (Lacepede). Although pelagic, this fish feeds on shellfish in shallow coastal waters. Photo by Allan Power. Santo, New Hebrides.

125. *Mulloidichthys auriflamma* (Forskal). The photographic light brings out the yellow coloration of these goatfishes. Note the red eyes. Photo by Allan Power. Santo, New Hebrides.

Family MULLIDAE
GOATFISHES

While diving around tropical reefs which have sandy patches in the vicinity, you probably will encounter goatfishes from time to time. It is quite a sight to see a small school of 25 to 50 individuals move over the sand searching for food with their barbels. As they vigorously manipulate their barbels over the sand they stir it up, but it soon becomes calm again after they leave. Once a small shrimp or crab is detected it is quickly eaten.

Goatfishes will often be encountered resting on the sand and at night may be seen, usually with a completely different color pattern, in the same sandy areas. Some of the photos on these pages show the nighttime coloration of goatfishes as well as their usual daytime livery.

Small goatfishes are well suited for aquaria. They stay on the bottom sand most of the time, picking up bits of food missed by the other fishes. They are normally not aggressive and are not bothered by too many of the other aquarium fishes.

Aside from the characteristic barbels, goatfishes have two separated dorsal fins, the first composed of about six to eight weak spines. The anal fin has only one or two spines, in contrast to most percoids which have three. The caudal fin is forked and the ventrals are thoracic in position.

Goatfishes have another common name, the surmullets. This name and the family name should not be confused with the true mullets of the family Mugilidae, which in turn should not be confused with the weevers of the family Mugiloididae.

Goatfishes are considered good food fishes and in certain areas may be highly prized for their flesh. In Hawaii the goatfishes are eagerly sought and bring a decent price in the market. Fresh goatfishes may be baked or roasted and served complete with fins and head, a practice that in some parts of our country would be frowned upon. The red surmullet, *Mullus surmuletus*, of Europe (especially the Mediterranean) is considered an excellent food fish.

126. *Mulloidichthys samoensis* (Gunther). A species closely related to *M. auriflamma* and difficult to differentiate from that species. Note the light-colored eyes. Photo by Allan Power. Santo, New Hebrides.

127. *Parupeneus bifasciatus* (Lacepede). A small group of goatfishes mingling with some damselfishes (*Abudefduf curacao*) among the coral. Photo by Allan Power. Santo, New Hebrides.

128. *Parupeneus bifasciatus* (Lacepede). The dark blotches on the sides may become solid bars at times. Photo by Dr. Herbert R. Axelrod. Marau, Br. Solomon Islands.

129. *Upeneus tragula* Richardson. On a sandy bottom the chin barbels are used to search for food. Here the sand is stirred up by these actions. Photo by Allan Power. Santo, New Hebrides.

130. *Parupeneus bifasciatus* (Lacepede). This species is generally encountered in shallow coastal waters. It grows to a length of almost one foot. Photo by Allan Power. Santo, New Hebrides.

131. *Mulloidichthys samoensis* (Gunther). The white pelvic fins help distinguish this fish from *M. auriflamma*, where they are yellow. This blotchy pattern may be its fright colors. Photo by Allan Power. Santo, New Hebrides.

132. *Parupeneus chryseredros* (Lacepede). The barbels can easily be seen on this individual. Note also the pattern of blue lines around the head. Photo by Aaron Norman.

133. *Parupeneus barberinus* (Lacepede). This is one of the larger goatfishes, growing to a length of about 20 inches. Photo by Dr. Herbert R. Axelrod. Marau, Br. Solomon Islands.

134. *Parupeneus* sp. (possibly *P. chryseredros*). Goatfishes reach sizes of a foot or more and in many areas are considered an excellent food fish. Photo by Dr. Herbert R. Axelrod. Marau, Br. Solomon Islands.

135. *Parupeneus* sp. (possibly *P. chryseredros*). The barbels are located on the end of the lower jaw. As food is detected, a quick snap of the jaws usually engulfs it. Photo by Dr. Herbert R. Axelrod. Marau, Br. Solomon Islands.

136. *?Anthias pleurotaenia* Bleeker. A colorful fish with a double stripe along its lower side. It has also been tentatively identified by one expert as *A. bimaculatus* Smith and by another as a new species. Photo by Dr. Herbert R. Axelrod. Marau, Br. Solomon Islands.

137. *?Anthias* sp. (probably close to *A. squamipinnis*). A male with two prolonged dorsal fin spines. Another *Anthias* can be seen head on in the background. Photo by Allan Power. Santo, New Hebrides.

138. *?Anthias pleurotaenia* Bleeker. In the several specimens pictured here the light colored squarish blotch on the side is always present. Photo by Dr. Herbert R. Axelrod. Marau, Br. Solomon Islands.

139. *?Anthias pleurotaenia* Bleeker. The classification of this group is very confused and is presently under study. Sexual dimorphism adds much to the confusion. Photo by Dr. Gerald R. Allen. Savo, Br. Solomon Islands.

140. *?Anthias hutchi* Bleeker. The generic classification is unsettled and some of these species might be placed in *Franzia*. Photo by Heiko Bleher. Marau, Br. Solomon Islands.

141. *?Anthias hutchi* Bleeker. Probably a male. Originally described from Ambon Island in the East Indies. Photo by Dr. Gerald Allen. Savo, Br. Solomon Islands (50 feet deep).

142. ?*Anthias pleurotaenia* Bleeker. Some specimens can only be captured by drastic means. This one was speared, as can be seen by the hole in its back. Photo by Dr. Herbert R. Axelrod. Marau, Br. Solomon Islands.

143. ?*Anthias pleurotaenia* Bleeker. A close-up of the head pattern. The eye to pectoral bar is found in many species of *Anthias*. Photo by Dr. Herbert R. Axelrod. Marau, Br. Solomon Islands.

144. ?*Anthias pleurotaenia* Bleeker. Much of the pattern is absent in this individual, but the purplish caudal fin tips and anal fin pattern remain. Photo by Dr. Herbert R. Axelrod. Marau, Br. Solomon Islands.

145. ?*Anthias hutchi* Bleeker. This young anthiid has not fully developed the elongate third dorsal spine. The eye to pectoral bar may either be undeveloped or temporarily faded. Photo by Dr. Gerald R. Allen. Guadalcanal, Br. Solomon Islands.

146. ?*Anthias hutchi* Bleeker. The dorsal spine and eye to pectoral stripe are both developed, and the fins are becoming more angular. Photo by Dr. Gerald R. Allen. Madang, New Guinea (20 feet deep).

147. *Mirolabrichthys dispar* Herre (center) and an unknown anthiid (below it) among the coral formations of Marau, Br. Solomon Islands. Photo by Heiko Bleher.

148. *Mirolabrichthys dispar* Herre. The photographer's flash caught the brilliant colors of this fish. Photo by Allan Power. Santo, New Hebrides.

149. *Mirolabrichthys dispar* Herre. Experts are not in agreement as to the identity of this fish. This one is caught in the act of "yawning." Photo by Allan Power. Santo, New Hebrides.

150. *Mirolabrichthys tuka* Herre and Montalban. Juvenile. This young individual looks very much like *M. evansi* (PMF-3, p. 648) but has less yellow. Photo by Dr. Herbert R. Axelrod. Marau, Br. Solomon Islands.

151. *Mirolabrichthys tuka* Herre and Montalban. Larger individuals of the same species on the reef. These 4-inch fish may be females. Photo by Dr. Gerald R. Allen. Guadalcanal, Br. Solomon Islands (60 feet deep).

152. *Mirolabrichthys tuka* Herre and Montalban. Possibly a young male. The semicircular notch in the anal fin is real and not the result of any damage. Photo by Dr. Herbert R. Axelrod. Marau, Br. Solomon Islands.

153. *Mirolabrichthys tuka* Herre and Montalban. Fully developed male. Traces of the orange or yellow stripe are visible along the back. Photo by Dr. Gerald R. Allen. Guadalcanal, Br. Solomon Islands (70 feet deep).

154. *Mirolabrichthys dispar* Herre and Montalban. A male (right) and what may be a small group of females (4 individuals). The dorsal fin of the 'females' is not as colorful. Photo by Allan Power. Santo, New Hebrides.

155. *Pseudochromis fuscus* Muller and Troschel. Most of the dorsal fin is composed of rays, only the first three elements being spines. Photo by Dr. Herbert R. Axelrod. Marau, Br. Solomon Islands.

156. *Pseudochromis fuscus* Muller and Troschel. This pseudochromid has made its home under a piece of branching coral. The aquarist might find one doing the same thing in his aquarium. Photo by Dr. Gerald R. Allen. Port Moresby, New Guinea (20 feet deep).

157. *Pseudochromis xanthochir* Bleeker. It is possible that this species is synonymous with *P. fuscus*. In *P. xanthochir* the fins are yellowish instead of dusky. Photo by Dr. Herbert R. Axelrod. Marau, Br. Solomon Islands.

158. *Pseudochromis paccagnellae* Axelrod. This little fish has turned up in many areas since its description. It is surprising that it has gone relatively unnoticed until recently. Photo by Heiko Bleher. Marau, Br. Solomon Islands.

159. *Pseudochromis paccagnellae* Axelrod. The white stripe dividing the two colors in the original specimen is all but absent in this one. Photo by Dr. Herbert R. Axelrod. Marau, Br. Solomon Islands.

160. *Pseudochromis paccagnellae* Axelrod. This fish has appeared for sale in local pet shops and seems to do well in aquaria. Photo by Dr. Herbert R. Axelrod. Marau, Br. Solomon Islands.

161. *Pseudochromis paccagnellae* Axelrod. Pseudochromids may take shelter in coral. If the coral piece is small enough the fish can be caught by picking it up and shaking the fish out. In deeper water put the coral into a net and bring everything up to the surface. Photo by Allan Power. Santo, New Hebrides.

162. *Pseudoplesiops sargeanti* Schultz. *Pseudoplesiops* is a genus of small fishes characterized by having all the dorsal and anal rays soft and flexible. Photo by Dr. Herbert R. Axelrod. Marau, Br. Solomon Islands.

163. *Plesiops coeruleolineatus* Ruppell. A pretty little fish usually found where wave action is relatively strong. Photo by Dr. Herbert R. Axelrod. Marau, Br. Solomon Islands.

164. *Liopropoma* sp. (possibly *L. pallidum*). Although this is one of the grouper allies, it bears a distinct resemblance to the cardinalfishes (Apogonidae). Photo by Dr. Herbert R. Axelrod. Marau, Br. Solomon Islands.

165. *Liopropoma* sp. This may be a new species of *Liopropoma*, but further investigation is needed before a description can be presented. Photo by Dr. Herbert R. Axelrod. Marau, Br. Solomon Islands.

166. *Liopropoma susumi* Jordan and Seale. This species is distinguished from the one below by having four dark stripes on the side of the caudal peduncle instead of five. Photo by Dr. Herbert R. Axelrod. Marau, Br. Solomon Islands.

167. *Liopropoma lineata* (Schultz). There are no reports about the ability of this fish to live in a home aquarium. From experience with related fishes it would be expected to do well. Photo by Dr. Herbert R. Axelrod. Marau, Br. Solomon Islands.

168. *Pseudogramma polyacantha* (Bleeker). A fairly common species tha grows to only about 2½ inches at maturity. Photo by Dr. Herbert R. Axelrod. Marau, Br. Solomon Islands.

169. *Grammistops ocellatus* Schultz. The first dorsal fin, which is folded back in this specimen, is composed of seven spines. This species remained unnamed until 1953. Photo by Dr. Herbert R. Axelrod. Marau, Br. Solomon Islands.

170. *Plectropomus oligacanthus* Bleeker. The combination of stripes anteriorly and spots posteriorly makes this species readily recognizable. Photo by Dr. Herbert R. Axelrod. Marau, Br. Solomon Islands.

171. *Plectropomus oligacanthus* Bleeker. Head and anterior body showing blue line pattern. This species reaches a length of about 2 feet. Photo by Dr. Herbert R. Axelrod. Marau, Br. Solomon Islands.

172. *Cephalopholis coatesi* Whitley. This species previously was known from Queensland, Australia and New Guinea and apparently ranges into the island chain of Melanesia. Photo by Dr. Herbert R. Axelrod. Marau, Br. Solomon Islands.

173. *Cephalopholis aurantius* (Valenciennes). Species of *Cephalopholis*, this one included, quickly outgrow most aquaria. Photo by Dr. Herbert R. Axelrod, Marau, Br. Solomon Islands.

174. *Cephalopholis aurantius* (Valenciennes). Close-up of head showing teeth and pattern of bluish spots on head. Photo by Dr. Herbert R. Axelrod. Marau, Br. Solomon Islands.

175. *Cephalopholis miniatus* (Forskal). The capacity of a groupers' mouth is exceeded only by its appetite. Photo by Dr. Herbert R. Axelrod. Marau, Br. Solomon Islands.

176. *Cephalopholis urodelus* (Schneider). The grouper eye usually has an extension or notch anteriorly to aid in binocular vision. Photo by Dr. Herbert R. Axelrod. Marau, Br. Solomon Islands.

177. *Cephalopholis urodelus* (Schneider). Small flag-tailed groupers or flag-tailed rock cods are easily kept in marine aquaria. Photo by Dr. Herbert R. Axelrod. Marau, Br. Solomon Islands.

178. *Cephalopholis leopardus* (Lacepede). This and other groupers welcome feedings of guppies and other small fishes. Photo by Dr. Herbert R. Axelrod. Marau, Br. Solomon Islands.

179. *Cephalopholis leopardus* (Lacepede). This very small specimen still has not developed the caudal fin pattern characteristic of the species. Photo by Dr. Herbert R. Axelrod. Marau, Br. Solomon Islands.

180. *Cephalopholis aurantius* (Valenciennes). Often confused with *C. sonnerati*, but that species has a network of blue lines on its head and black edges to its fins. Photo by Dr. Herbert R. Axelrod. Marau, Br. Solomon Islands.

181. *Cephalopholis miniatus* (Forskal). The cleaning wrasse, *Labroides dimidiatus*, is working on the side of this grouper while a cleaning shrimp, *Stenopus hispidus,* waits off to the right. Little or no data are available on whether or not the two types of cleaners will actually work on one fish at the same time. Photo by Allan Power. Santo, New Hebrides.

182. *Epinephelus fario* (Thunberg). Groupers and other fishes too large for the photo tank must be photographed on the deck or a suitable background. Photo by Dr. Herbert R. Axelrod. Marau, Br. Solomon Islands.

183. *Plectropomus leopardus* (Lacepede). Most species of *Plectropomus* have some pattern of blue spots and are difficult to separate. This 12-inch individual roughly fits the description of *P. truncatus*, but the spots are not numerous enough. Photo by Dr. Gerald R. Allen. Espiritu Santo, New Hebrides (30 feet deep).

184. *Cephalopholis pachycentron* (Valenciennes). There may be about six to eight dark vertical bars on the body (faintly visible in this photo) at times. Note the blue and reddish-brown pattern in the fins. Photo by Allan Power. Santo, New Hebrides.

185. *Epinephelus fasciatus* (Forskal). The delicate coloration of this grouper has made it a popular aquarium fish. Photo by Pierre Laboute. New Caledonia.

186. As the grouper *Epinephelus merra* Bloch swims over the sea urchin bed, the smaller fishes (mostly apogonids) dart safely about among the spines. When the grouper is gone they will come out again. Photo by Pierre Laboute. New Caledonia.

187. *Variola louti* (Forskal). The crescent-shaped caudal fin is characteristic and has gained this fish the name of lyretail grouper. Photo by Allan Power. Santo, New Hebrides.

Family NEMIPTERIDAE
BUTTERFLY-BREAM

The two most important genera of this family are *Nemipterus* and *Scolopsis*. The species of *Nemipterus* are generally referred to as butterfly-bream, whereas the species of *Scolopsis* are more commonly referred to as the monocle-bream. The monocle-bream are distinguishable from *Nemipterus* by having a prominent posteriorly directed spine below the eye.

Scolopsids are generally smallish fishes, few growing larger than 12 inches. They are suitable for marine aquaria, and a few species, *Scolopsis bilineatus* for example, are seen from time to time in pet shops.

Identification of the species involves number of scales, proportions, and color pattern. Aquarists can be fairly certain of the identity of these fishes on color pattern alone although there may be slight problems in recognizing juveniles. The most distinctive species, *Scolopsis bilineatus*, also has a yellow phase according to Dr. Gerald R. Allen, who photographed it in the Fiji Islands.

Like many other fishes, scolopsids will sleep on the reef among the coral or rocks. While in this position they change their color pattern, usually becoming blotchy in appearance.

The genus *Ctenoscolopsis* differs from *Scolopsis* only by having a denticulated ridge along the upper border of the maxillary bone and may eventually be synonymized with that genus. The species found in Melanesia, *C. ciliatus*, is quite attractive, with bright yellow eyes and lateral spots and a silver or white streak along the back, all on a blue-gray background. This species should do well in the aquarium trade.

Scolopsids have a single continuous dorsal fin of about ten spines and nine rays, and an anal fin of three spines and six to seven rays. The spines in both fins are weak. The mouth is moderate in size and the jaws are provided with slender curved teeth in bands, the outer row enlarged. The palate is toothless.

188. *Ctenoscolopsis ciliatus* (Lacepede). The silver streak along the back (there may be a second streak in the young) and bright yellow spots on the sides make this fish easily identifiable. Photo by Allan Power. Santo, New Hebrides.

189. *Ctenoscolopsis ciliatus* (Lacepede) and *Upeneus tragula* Richardson over a sandy spot on the reef. The flash fades quickly with distance underwater. Photo by Allan Power. Santo, New Hebrides.

190. *Scolopsis bilineatus* (Bloch). The typical color pattern of a two-lined snapper as it swims about the reef. Photo by Allan Power. Santo, New Hebrides.

191. *Scolopsis bilineatus* (Bloch). At night or when frightened the color changes dramatically. The characteristic two curved lines are still present. Note the white triangular spot below the soft dorsal fin in both photos. Photo by Allan Power. Santo, New Hebrides.

192. *Scolopsis margaritifer* (Cuvier). A coastal fish reaching a size of about 10 inches. This one is only about 6 inches long. Photo by Dr. Gerald R. Allen. Madang, New Guinea.

193. *Scolopsis cancellatus* (Cuvier). The white stripes may become connected posteriorly by narrow cross stripes. Photo of a 6-inch individual by Dr. Gerald R. Allen. Florida Island, Br. Solomon Islands (4 feet deep).

194. *Scolopsis margaritifer* (Cuvier). Another color phase of the pearly snapper. The upper caudal fin lobe and much of the ventral part of the fish are yellow. Photo by Dr. Herbert R. Axelrod. Marau, Br. Solomon Islands.

195. *Scolopsis bilineatus* (Bloch). The large eye and the head shape are generally characteristic of the species of the genus *Scolopsis*. Photo by Dr. Herbert R. Axelrod. Marau, Br. Solomon Islands.

196. *Scolopsis xenochrous* Gunther. A pretty little fish that rarely if ever is seen in marine aquarium stores. It attains a length of only 8 to 9 inches. Photo by Dr. Herbert R. Axelrod. Marau, Br. Solomon Islands.

197. *Scolopsis margaritifer* (Cuvier). The dark lateral stripe is only hinted at in previous photos (pp. 1496-97) but is very evident in this 4-inch specimen. Photo by Dr. Gerald R. Allen. Port Moresby, New Guinea.

198. The night coloration of this scolopsid makes it difficult to identify. It probably is *Scolopsis cancellatus* since faint light stripes are visible in the upper side. Photo by Allan Power. Santo, New Hebrides.

199. *Scolopsis xenochrous* Gunther. Scolopsids are not difficult to keep in home aquaria providing plenty of space and good food are available. Photo by Dr. Gerald R. Allen of a 5-inch fish from Guadalcanal, Br. Solomon Islands.

200. *Scolopsis bilineatus* (Bloch). According to Dr. Allen, young *S. bilineatus* may take on this bright yellow color. Photo of a 3-inch individual by Dr. Gerald R. Allen. Suva, Fiji Islands (6 feet deep).

201. *Gnathodentex aurolineatus* (Lacepede). Apparently disturbed by the photographer-diver, this spot bream is changing from its night coloration to the normal daytime color. Photo by Heiko Bleher. Marau, Br. Solomon Islands.

202. *Gnathodentex aureolineatus* (Lacepede). The spot bream (or gold-lined sea-bream as it is sometimes called) attains a length of about 1½ feet. Photo by Dr. Herbert R. Axelrod. Marau, Br. Solomon Islands.

203. *Monotaxis grandoculis* (Forskal). The large-eyed bream is encountered mostly along coastal waters near reefs. Photo by Dr. Herbert R. Axelrod. Marau, Br. Solomon Islands.

204. A young *Scolopsis* that has not developed the recognizable adult color pattern. Photo by Dr. Herbert R. Axelrod. Marau, Br. Solomon Islands.

205. *Pentapodus caninus* (Cuvier). Pentapodids are closely related to the scolopsids and are usually included in the same family. Photo of a 6-inch individual by Dr. Gerald R. Allen. Florida Island, Br. Solomon Islands (5 feet deep).

206. *Pentapodus nemurus* (Bleeker). The lobes of the caudal fin are usually prolonged into filaments. In this specimen they have not yet developed or were damaged during capture. Photo by Aaron Norman.

207. *Pterocaesio tile* (Cuvier and Valenciennes). At night most species of fusiliers exhibit a different color than they do during the daytime. This fish was photographed at night by photoflash. Photo by Dr. Herbert R. Axelrod. Marau, Br. Solomon Islands.

208. *Caesio cuning* (Bloch). As in many of the species of *Caesio*, the color patterns may change from one moment to another. This species may have the lower portion of the body a bright rosy color. Photo by Allan Power. Santo, New Hebrides.

209. A young *Caesio*, possibly *C. pisang*. The colors will probably intensify so that the caudal fin will be bright red with dark tips. Photo by Dr. Herbert R. Axelrod. Marau, Br. Solomon Islands.

210. A school of fusiliers which appear to be a mixture of three species. The reddish one is *Caesio pisang*, the common deep-bodied blue species may be *Caesio chrysozonus*, and the slender-bodied blue species may be a species of *Gymnocaesio*. Photo by Allan Power. Santo, New Hebrides.

211. *Pterocaesio tile* (Cuvier and Valenciennes). With the dorsal and anal fins folded back these fishes present a very streamlined appearance. Photo by Pierre Laboute. New Caledonia.

212. *?Caesio pulcherrimus* Smith. This species was described from Assumption Island in the western Indian Ocean. A similar species from our area has the yellow extending to the snout. Photo by Allan Power. Santo, New Hebrides.

213. *Gaterin orientalis* (Bloch). Hobbyists often keep this species in their home aquaria. It is colorful and hardy. Photo by Dr. Herbert R. Axelrod. Marau, Br. Solomon Islands.

214. *Gaterin chaetodonoides* (Lacepede). Each clown sweetlips seems to have its own distinctive variation of its basic pattern. The white areas in this juvenile and those on the following pages are all in approximately the same places, however. Photo of a 5-inch individual by Dr. Gerald R. Allen. Efate, New Hebrides (30 feet deep).

Family **POMADASYIDAE**
GRUNTS, SWEETLIPS, ETC.

It is generally considered that the sweetlips or thick-lipped grunts should be included in the family Pomadasyidae. The differences between the two groups are apparently not great enough to continue the use of family Gaterinidae (or Plectorhynchidae). Gaterins have thick lips, by which they can easily be recognized and from which the common name was derived. They usually have smaller scales than other grunts, but there is an overlap with some species of grunts.

Most species of gaterins can be found around coral reefs or even entering estuaries. They range throughout most of the Indo-Pacific (but have not been reported from the Hawaiian Islands or the East Pacific) and are absent from the Atlantic Ocean.

Sweetlips are omnivorous, eating a variety of foods. They will probably do well on fish, clams, squids, crustaceans, etc., but adding some vegetable matter to their diet might give them a treat.

The changes occurring with growth have been a source of confusion for scientists. It is only when a full series (large and small specimens plus all the intermediate stages) has been accumulated that the proper name of the species can be arrived at. Aquarists have the advantage here in that they can watch the changes as their fish grows and there is no doubt which adult pattern belongs with which juvenile pattern.

The peculiar swimming motion of the juveniles has been mentioned before, but it might be interesting to add here that this swimming motion is similar in some aspects to the anemonefishes and some small angelfishes. No reasons for this type of swimming have been reported. Usually it means that the fish is a cleaner or is mimicking something for protection.

215. *Gaterin chaetodonoides* (Lacepede). This fish is larger than the one opposite and the juvenile color pattern is starting to break up into the spotted pattern. Photo by Allan Power. Santo, New Hebrides.

216. *Gaterin orientalis* (Bloch). The changes occurring as gaterins grow to maturity have caused many problems in the classification of these fishes. Some of these problems are still not resolved. Photo by Allan Power. Santo, New Hebrides.

217. *Gaterin chaetodonoides* (Lacepede). Young clown sweetlips are the favorites of marine aquarists in this group of fishes. They can be fed on fish, clams, squid, etc., a diet which will put inches on their length. Photo by Dr. Herbert R. Axelrod.

218. *Gaterin chaetodonoides* (Lacepede). Adult. It is no wonder that this fish and the one above were at first thought to be different species. This fish is about a foot or a foot and a half long compared to the 4-5 inches long fish above. Photo by Pierre Laboute. New Caledonia.

219. *Gaterin orientalis* (Bloch). Underwater photographs really show the fishes at their best. It is up to the aquarist to try and imitate or substitute for the natural conditions and food in order to keep them happy. Photo by Allan Power. Santo, New Hebrides.

220. *Gaterin goldmanni* (Bleeker). The young of this species is said to have about nine horizontal stripes (increasing to 18-19 with age). The upper stripes become as seen in this photo and the lower stripes break up into spots and eventually disappear. Photo by Pierre Laboute. New Caledonia.

221. *Gaterin picus* (Cuvier and Valenciennes). One of the few gaterins in which at least parts of the juvenile pattern are retained by the adult. The young stage is pictured in PMF-5, p. 1273. Photo by Allan Power. Santo, New Hebrides.

222. *Spilotichthys pictus* (Thunberg). Fishes are generally wary of a diver, but they are often also curious. The closest fish has not moved away but is keeping a wary eye on the photographer. Photo by Pierre Laboute. New Caledonia.

223. *Spilotichthys pictus* (Thunberg). All the fins of a fish are used in maneuvering. Here they are set for a turn. Photo by Allan Power. Santo, New Hebrides.

224. *Lethrinus* sp. This is one of the short-snouted species of lethrinid. The front part of the dorsal fin is folded back so that the soft dorsal and anal fins appear equal in area. Photo by Allan Power. Santo, New Hebrides.

225. *Lethrinus chrysostomus* Richardson? One of the longer snouted species. It resembles the Indian Ocean form *L. xanthocheilus* illustrated in PMF-5, 1301. Photo by Pierre Laboute. New Caledonia.

226. *Lutjanus lutjanus* Bloch? A snapper caught sleeping by the photographer's flash. Note the night coloration. Photo by Allan Power. Santo, New Hebrides.

227. *Lutjanus kasmira* (Forskal). This is probably the most popular of the snappers in marine aquarists' tanks. Photo by Heiko Bleher. Marau, Br. Solomon Islands.

228. *Lutjanus kasmira* (Forskal). The four black-lined blue stripes characteristic of this species are clearly visible in this photo. Photo by Dr. Herbert R. Axelrod. Marau, Br. Solomon Islands.

229. *Lutjanus bohar* (Forskal). This snapper attains a length of about two feet or more. Photo by Dr. Herbert R. Axelrod. Marau, Br. Solomon Islands.

230. *Lutjanus quinquelineatus* (Bloch). A school of five-lined snappers. This species can easily be distinguished from the four-lined snappers on the opposite page by the extra stripe. Photo by Pierre Laboute. New Caledonia.

231. *Lutjanus gibbus* (Forskal). This red snapper has received the common name "paddle-tail" because the upper caudal fin lobe becomes enlarged with age. Photo by Dr. Herbert R. Axelrod. Marau, Br. Solomon Islands.

232. *Lutjanus gibbus* (Forskal). The preoperculum is deeply notched in this species. Photo by Dr. Herbert R. Axelrod. Marau, Br. Solomon Islands.

233. *Lutjanus sebae* (Cuvier). Even head-on the emperor snapper is easily recognizable. Photo by Dr. Herbert R. Axelrod. Marau, Br. Solomon Islands.

234. *Macolor* sp. This apparently new species was collected in the Solomon Islands. Unfortunately the specimen was lost and it must remain unnamed (or unidentified) until more specimens are found. Photo by Dr. Herbert R. Axelrod. Marau, Br. Solomon Islands.

235. *Macolor* sp. The obvious differences between this species and the similarly patterned *Macolor niger* (see PMF-5, p. 1276) are in the fins. The saddle-shaped dorsal fin, the hyaline pectoral fins, and the elongated pelvic fins are not found in *M. niger*. Photo of a 3-inch specimen by Dr. Gerald R. Allen. Malaita, Br. Solomon Islands (50 feet deep).

Family CHAETODONTIDAE
BUTTERFLYFISHES

Many of the butterflyfishes found in Melanesia are also found throughout the tropical Pacific. Familiar species such as *Chaetodon ephippium* and *C. ornatissimus* have wide ranges and might be encountered wherever butterflyfishes are found. *Chaetodon kleini*, probably one of the commonest of the butterflyfishes, and one which occurs over two oceans, appears in pet shops regularly, but because of its subdued coloration is not very popular. It is probably one of the hardiest of the butterflyfishes, and anybody who wants to keep them might well start with a *kleini*.

Chaetodon pelewensis is presented here for the first time and is a southern Pacific Ocean species. It is closely related to *C. punctatofasciatus* but differs from that species in the positioning of the blackish stripes. Another butterflyfish that makes its first appearance here but should be covered more fully in the next volume is *Chaetodon flavirostris*. One of the intermediate stages is shown in photo #244, the adult being duskier and having some orange markings on the head instead of the white. This species is found only in the southwestern tropical Pacific.

Butterflyfishes rest at night among the corals and take on a darkened appearance. For example, *Chaetodon vagabundus* will have a large indistinct dark blotch on its side below the middle of the dorsal fin. Others may have a similar spot, several blotches, or other distinct nighttime pattern. Collectors who have been frustrated by the agility of butterflyfishes during the day may have a much easier time netting them at night. But remember, it is much more dangerous to dive at night.

236. *Chaetodon pelewensis* Kner. The black stripes of this fish are usually more uniform and slant from the soft dorsal fin toward the ventrals. Photo by Heiko Bleher. Marau, Br. Solomon Islands.

237. *Chaetodon ephippium* Cuvier. Butterflyfishes usually pose for photographers so that excellent photos such as this one can be taken. Photo by Allan Power. Santo, New Hebrides.

238. *Chaetodon ornatissimus* Cuvier. Ornate or clown butterflyfishes are almost always found in pairs. The companion to this one is probably not far away. Photo by Allan Power. Santo, New Hebrides.

239. *Chaetodon kleini* Bloch. This butterflyfish is picking at some food item on the outside of the shell of a bivalve mollusc. Photo by Heiko Bleher. Marau, Br. Solomon Islands.

240. *Chaetodon kleini* Bloch. The banded pattern usually seen in this species has almost faded in this specimen. Photo by Dr. Herbert R. Axelrod. Marau, Br. Solomon Islands.

241. *Chaetodon kleini* Bloch. A 5-inch individual (just about fully grown) at a depth of 30 feet. Photo by Dr. Gerald R. Allen. Efate, New Hebrides.

242. *Chaetodon kleini* Bloch. A typical *kleini* color pattern. This is what your fish should look like in your aquarium. Photo by Allan Power. Santo, New Hebrides.

243. *Chaetodon trifascialis* Quoy and Gaimard. Juvenile. These butterflyfish are generally 'loners' and patrol a definite territory. Photo by Dr. Herbert R. Axelrod. Marau, Br. Solomon Islands.

244. *Chaetodon flavirostris* Gunther. This young fish is intermediate between the juvenile and adult stages. Photo by Dr. Herbert R. Axelrod. Marau, Br. Solomon Islands.

245. *Chaetodon unimaculatus* Bloch. The large spot on the side may become more teardrop shaped, especially in Hawaiian populations. Photo by Dr. Herbert R. Axelrod. Marau, Br. Solomon Islands.

246. *Coradion altivelis* McCulloch. Juvenile, still with the dorsal fin spot. This spot fades with age. Photo by Dr. Herbert R. Axelrod. Marau, Br. Solomon Islands.

247. *Chaetodon baronessa* Cuvier. A diver can come very near a butterflyfish underwater if he is slow and careful not to frighten it. Photo by Allan Power. Santo, New Hebrides.

248. *Chaetodon trifasciatus* Mungo Park. The juvenile is colored somewhat differently than the adults. Compare this juvenile with the photos below and opposite. Photo by Dr. Herbert R. Axelrod. Marau, Br. Solomon Islands.

249. *Chaetodon trifasciatus* Mungo Park. Adult. Like *C. ornatissimus,* this species is rarely seen alone. It almost always has a companion. Photo by Allan Power. Santo, New Hebrides.

250. *Chaetodon trifasciatus* Mungo Park. Adult. This species does not grow very large. It is also one of the most difficult to keep in home aquaria. Photo by Dr. Herbert R. Axelrod. Marau, Br. Solomon Islands.

251. *Chaetodon vagabundus* Linnaeus. At night this species has a dark blotch on the upper back as shown here. Photo by Allan Power. Santo, New Hebrides.

252. *Chaetodon ulietensis* Cuvier. This species usually is found in small groups as seen here. Photo by Pierre Laboute. New Caledonia.

253. *Heniochus chrysostomus* Cuvier. This fish was just within reach of the flash. Photo by Dr. Herbert R. Axelrod. Marau, Br. Solomon Islands.

254. *Heniochus chrysostomus* Cuvier. This fish, also normally found in pairs, is often found under or near ledges or caves. Photo by Allan Power. Santo, New Hebrides.

255. *Forcipiger flavissimus* Jordan and McGregor. The extremely long and falcate pectoral fins are unusual in butterflyfishes. Photo by Dr. Herbert R. Axelrod. Marau, Br. Solomon Islands.

256. *Forcipiger flavissimus* Jordan and McGregor. The dorsal spines are raised as a protective device or threat. Photo by Allan Power. Santo, New Hebrides.

257. *Platax pinnatus* (Linnaeus). Only 4 inches long, this individual is probably over 9 inches high. Photo by Dr. Gerald R. Allen. Guadalcanal, Br. Solomon Islands (10 feet deep).

258. *Platax teira* (Forskal). At 7 inches in length the fins are still extremely elongate in this species. Photo by Dr. Gerald R. Allen. Madang, New Guinea (10 feet deep).

259. *Apolemichthys trimaculatus* (Lacepede). The long, sharp preopercular spine stands out against the yellow color of this angelfish. Photo by Dr. Herbert R. Axelrod. Marau, Br. Solomon Islands.

260. *Platax pinnatus* (Linnaeus). Adult. The snout is produced and the color pattern has drastically changed from the younger fish. Photo by Allan Power. Santo, New Hebrides.

261. *Pygoplites diacanthus* (Boddaert). A photo of a juvenile with the dark ocellated spot in its dorsal fin. Photo by Dr. Herbert R. Axelrod. Marau, Br. Solomon Islands.

262. *Euxiphipops navarchus* (Cuvier and Valenciennes). One of the favorites of the marine aquarist but commanding a fairly high price. Photo of a 10-inch individual by Dr. Gerald R. Allen. Madang, New Guinea (30 feet deep).

263. *Euxiphipops xanthometapon* (Bleeker). The fine teeth are used for scraping algae and nipping off small bits of food. Photo by Allan Power. Santo, New Hebrides.

264. *Pomacanthus semicirculatus* (Cuvier and Valenciennes). Only large public aquaria can house fully grown Koran angelfishes. Photo by Allan Power. Santo, New Hebrides.

265. *Pygloplites diacanthus* (Boddaert). The striped pattern sometimes has some anomalies in it. Here one of the yellow stripes is incomplete. Photo by Heiko Bleher. Marau, Br. Solomon Islands.

266. *Pomacanthus semicirculatus* (Cuvier and Valenciennes). The light area in the central portion of this fish is usually present and is not an artifact of photographic lighting. Photo by Pierre Laboute. New Caledonia.

267. *Pomacanthus imperator* (Bloch). Angelfishes are easy to photograph. They allow you to come very close and usually present their profile. Photo by Allan Power. Santo, New Hebrides.

268. Four juveniles of angelfishes. Top left: *Pomacanthus imperator* (Bloch); top right: *Pomacanthus imperator* (Bloch) but with incomplete white rings; bottom left: *Pomacanthus semicirculatus* (Cuvier and Valenciennes); bottom right: *Euxiphipops xanthometapon* (Bleeker). Photos by Dr. D. Terver, Nancy Aquarium, France.

269. *Centropyge bicolor* (Bloch). Several common names have been applied to this species, among them oriole angelfish, black-and-yellow angelfish, and bicolored angelfish. Photo by Dr. Herbert R. Axelrod. Marau, Br. Solomon Islands.

270. *Centropyge bicolor* (Bloch). Although sometimes called the black-and-yellow angelfish, it is definitely a blue-and-yellow pattern. Photo of a 5-inch specimen by Dr. Gerald R. Allen. Madang, New Guinea (20 feet deep).

271. *Centropyge bicolor* (Bloch). Oriole angelfishes are usually difficult to keep in home aquaria. Photo by Allan Power. Santo, New Hebrides.

272. *Centropyge vroliki* (Bleeker). The pearl-scaled angelfish is very hard to photograph. It turns brownish when disturbed (as it is here while being photographed). Photo by Dr. Herbert R. Axelrod. Marau, Br. Solomon Islands.

273. *Centropyge multifasciatus* (Smith and Radcliffe). This small angelfish is usually seen in relatively deep water. Photo by Dr. Herbert R. Axelrod. Marau, Br. Solomon Islands.

274. *Centropyge flavissimus* Cuvier. The species of *Centropyge* act like damselfishes when approached and peer out at the intruder from the cover of coral branches. Photo by Allan Power. Santo, New Hebrides.

275. *Genicanthus lamarck* (Lacepede). Another deeper water angelfish that rarely enters the aquarium trade. Photo by Dr. Herbert R. Axelrod. Marau, Br. Solomon Islands.

276. *Genicanthus melanospilus* (Bleeker). Female. The angelfishes in this genus show sexual dichromatism; that is, they can be sexed through differences in color pattern. Photo of a 5-inch individual by Dr. Gerald R. Allen. Espiritu Santo, New Hebrides (50 feet deep).

Family POMACENTRIDAE
ANEMONEFISHES AND DAMSELFISHES

Dr. Gerald R. Allen, who has provided many excellent photos for this book, has been working for several years on the classification of the pomacentrids. His reclassification of the anemonefishes has helped straighten out many of the inconsistencies in the names applied to these fishes. He has now turned his talents to the damselfishes, and most of the identifications in this section (as far as species names are concerned) have been made or confirmed by him. The generic names used here by us are the ones most commonly used in current literature. As Dr. Allen's work progresses, he is dividing the species into more natural groups and has to shift some of the species around a bit. When he is finished there will be a number of different generic names applied to the damsels.

In reviewing his work on the anemonefishes he has decided to return to the use of *Premnas biaculeatus* instead of *Amphiprion biaculeatus*, which was used in his revision. Although there is only one species in the genus *Premnas*, it is an interesting one. The two large sharp spines below each eye set it apart from the other anemonefishes. The color of these fishes seems variable, ranging from orange to reddish to a dark brown. *Premnas biaculeatus* is readily available in marine fish stores, and prices are usually not high.

Only one species of anemonefish has so far shown indications of sexual dimorphism. *Amphiprion perideraion* males have orange edges to the upper and lower parts of the caudal fin; females lack this color. Both sexes are illustrated here.

Some of the damselfishes are shown here for the first time (at least one is a new species) and others may look familiar but are sporting unfamiliar names. As progress is made in the study of these fishes there should be fewer and fewer changes and the damselfish classification should become more stable so that aquarists will not have to relearn the names of their favorite species. Regardless of how many times a fish has its name changed, its care and feeding remain the same.

277. *Amphiprion melanopus* Bleeker. A *Labroides dimidiatus* is giving this fish the once-over for parasites. Photo by Allan Power. Santo, New Hebrides.

278. *Premnas biaculeatus* (Bloch). The enlarged double spine below the eye is the main character which separates *Premnas* from *Amphiprion*. Photo by Dr. Herbert R. Axelrod. Marau, Br. Solomon Islands.

279. *Premnas biaculeatus* (Bloch). This is the result of the operation shown on p. 1389 in front of this book. Photo by Dr. Herbert R. Axelrod. Marau, Br. Solomon Islands.

280. *Premnas biaculeatus* (Bloch). A dark brown version of the species shown on the opposite page. Photo by Dr. Herbert R. Axelrod. Marau, Br. Solomon Islands.

281. *Amphiprion chrysopterus* Cuvier. Two individuals in the transformation stages before the final adult color pattern. Note the changes in the soft dorsal and caudal fins. The butterflyfish in the background is *Chaetodon flavirostris*. Photo by Dr. Herbert R. Axelrod. Marau, Br. Solomon Islands.

282. *Amphiprion clarkii?* An adult and juvenile (small fish to the left of the adult) sharing an anemone. Photo by Heiko Bleher. Marau, Br. Solomon Islands.

283. *Amphiprion perideraion* Bleeker. Male with the reddish or orange borders to the caudal fin. Photo by Dr. Herbert R. Axelrod. Marau, Br. Solomon Islands.

284. *Amphiprion clarkii* (Bennett). A very atypical color pattern for this species. Photo by Pierre Laboute. New Caledonia.

285. *Amphiprion perideraion* Bleeker. Female without the reddish or orange borders to the caudal fin. Photo by Dr. Herbert R. Axelrod. Marau, Br. Solomon Islands.

286. *Amphiprion perideraion* Bleeker. The white stripe does not reach the lips, and the snout itself is of a pale color. Photo by Allan Power. Santo, New Hebrides.

287. *Amphiprion perideraion* Bleeker. This anemone was apparently disturbed and is contracting. The anemonefishes hover nearby. Photo by Allan Power. Santo, New Hebrides.

288. *Amphiprion clarkii* (Bennett). In this individual the usual white band around the caudal peduncle is missing. Photo by Dr. Herbert R. Axelrod. Marau, Br. Solomon Islands.

289. *Amphiprion melanopus* Bleeker. In *melanopus* the pelvic and anal fins are normally blackish. This is a typical color pattern. Photo by Dr. Herbert R. Axelrod. Marau, Br. Solomon Islands.

290. *Amphiprion chrysopterus* Cuvier. This species normally does not have the blackish pelvic and anal fins as shown here, but the identity has been confirmed by Dr. Gerald R. Allen, world authority on anemonefishes. Photo by Dr. Herbert R. Axelrod. Marau, Br. Solomon Islands.

291. *Amphiprion melanopus* Bleeker. The best photos of fishes are close ups using flash. Either a close up or telephoto lens can achieve this effect. Photo by Allan Power. Santo, New Hebrides.

292. *Dascyllus melanurus* Bleeker. Three damsels wait their turn at a *Labroides* cleaning station. The wrasse is almost as big as the fishes being cleaned. Photo by Heiko Bleher. Marau, Br. Solomon Islands.

293. *Dascyllus trimaculatus* (Ruppell). A very good fish for the beginning marine aquarist. It is hardy and adjusts well to captivity. Photo by Dr. Herbert R. Axelrod. Marau, Br. Solomon Islands.

294. *Chromis analis* (Cuvier). Species of *Chromis*, being more open water fishes, do not fare as well in aquaria. Photo by Dr. Herbert R. Axelrod. Marau, Br. Solomon Islands.

295. *Chromis margaritifer* Fowler. There are several species of damsels which are bicolored like this one. One of them is even found in the Caribbean. Photo by Dr. Herbert R. Axelrod. Marau, Br. Solomon Islands.

296. *Chromis amboinensis* Bleeker. This little damsel has long filaments on each tip of the caudal fin. Photo by Dr. Herbert R. Axelrod. Marau, Br. Solomon Islands.

297. *Pomacentrus popei* Jordan and Seale. The pale line extending into the anal fin along the ventral portion of the fish is one of the identifying characteristics. Photo by Dr. Herbert R. Axelrod. Marau, Br. Solomon Islands.

298. *Pomacentrus coelestis* Jordan and Starks. Blue damsels flash through the coral and rocks, adding some bright color to the reef. Photo by Allan Power. Santo, New Hebrides.

299. *Chromis lineatus* Fowler and Bean. There are very few horizontally striped damselfishes. Note also the filaments on the tips of the caudal fin. Photo by Dr. Herbert R. Axelrod. Marau, Br. Solomon Islands.

300. *Chromis lepidolepis* Bleeker. This species apparently ranges from Taiwan to Melanesia, including the East Indies. Photo by Dr. Herbert R. Axelrod. Marau, Br. Solomon Islands.

301. *Chromis atripes* Fowler and Bean. This fish is similar to the one above, but it lacks the dark bars along the outer edge of the caudal fin. Photo by Dr. Herbert R. Axelrod. Marau, Br. Solomon Islands.

302. *Chromis xanthurus* (Bleeker). This white-tailed damselfish occurs from the East Indies and the Philippines to Melanesia. Photo by Dr. Herbert R. Axelrod. Marau, Br. Solomon Islands.

303. *Chromis rollandi* Whitley. Brine shrimp is an excellent food for small damsels. They will usually take other types of prepared foods almost as eagerly. Photo by Dr. Herbert R. Axelrod. Marau, Br. Solomon Islands.

304. *Pomacentrus notophthalmus* Bleeker. Similar in pattern to the above, but note the black area around the vent. The green algae in the area is *Halimeda*. Photo by Heiko Bleher. Marau, Br. Solomon Islands.

305. *Acanthochromis polyacanthus* (Bleeker). It is very unusual in the damselfishes to see a stripe broken up into spots such as this one. Photo by Dr. Herbert R. Axelrod. Marau, Br. Solomon Islands.

306. *Acanthochromis polyacanthus* (Bleeker). The above-mentioned stripe has disappeared in this portrait. Photo by Dr. Herbert R. Axelrod. Marau, Br. Solomon Islands.

307. *Abudefduf leucogaster* (Bleeker). Damselfishes can almost always be found where there are rocky or coral areas on or near the reef. Photo by Heiko Bleher. Marau, Br. Solomon Islands.

308. *Abudefduf dickii* (Lienard). The bright yellow pectoral fin easily distinguishes this fish from *Abudefduf* (*Plectroglyphidodon*) *johnstonianus*, where it is clear. Photo by Dr. Herbert R. Axelrod. Marau, Br. Solomon Islands.

309. *Pomacentrus bankanensis* Bleeker. A very pretty little damselfish that occasionally is imported from the Philippines. Photo by Dr. Herbert R. Axelrod. Marau, Br. Solomon Islands.

310. *Pomacentrus bankanensis* Bleeker. This is the same species as above although it appears less colorful. Photo by Dr. Herbert R. Axelrod. Marau, Br. Solomon Islands.

311. *Pomacentrus perspicillatus* Cuvier. There is a dark ocellus at the base of the dorsal fin that is included in the larger dark spot that extends onto the side. Photo by Dr. Herbert R. Axelrod. Marau, Br. Solomon Islands.

312. *Pomacentrus perspicillatus* Cuvier. An older individual of the same species as above. Another dark mark is indicated in the anterior part of the spinous dorsal fin. Photo by Dr. Herbert R. Axelrod. Marau, Br. Solomon Islands.

313. *Pomacentrus nigromarginatus* Allen. This species is known throughout Melanesia plus the East Indies and the Great Barrier Reef of Australia. Photo by Dr. Herbert R. Axelrod. Marau, Br. Solomon Islands.

314. *Abudefduf whitleyi* Allen and Robertson. This species was described only recently (1974) from New Caledonia and the Great Barrier Reef of Australia. Photo by Allan Power. Santo, New Hebrides.

315. *Chromis* sp. Another new species, but this one doesn't have a name yet. It apparently was taken in deep water (110 feet), and that is why it hasn't been described until now. Photo by Dr. Gerald R. Allen. Suva, Fiji Islands.

316. *Pomacentrus coelestis* Jordan and Starks. Juvenile. This species has a common name of neon damsel because of the bright shining blue color exhibited on the reef. Photo of a juvenile by Dr. Herbert R. Axelrod. Marau, Br. Solomon Islands.

317. *Pomacentrus reidi* Fowler and Bean. Reid's damselfish attains a length of about 4½ to 5 inches. Photo by Dr. Herbert R. Axelrod. Marau, Br. Solomon Islands.

318. *Pomacentrus reidi* Fowler and Bean. This species was described from specimens from the Philippines and will occasionally be imported from there. Photo by Dr. Herbert R. Axelrod. Marau, Br. Solomon Islands.

319. *Pomacentrus lepidogenys* Fowler and Bean. A shallow water fish that feeds on plankton. Brine shrimp might be an excellent substitute food. Photo by Dr. Herbert R. Axelrod. Marau, Br. Solomon Islands.

320. *Chromis* sp. This undescribed species may be identical to the one on a previous page (photo #315). Photo by Dr. Herbert R. Axelrod. Marau, Br. Solomon Islands.

321. *Pomacentrus alexanderae* Evermann and Seale. Mostly found in Melanesia but extending into the East Indies, Philippines, and to the Great Barrier Reef. It was originally discovered in the Philippines. Photo by Dr. Herbert R. Axelrod. Marau, Br. Solomon Islands.

322. *Abudefduf aureus* (Cuvier). Dr. Gerald R. Allen has divided the pomacentrids into several genera. This species he places in genus *Amblyglyphidodon.* Photo by Dr. Herbert R. Axelrod. Marau, Br. Solomon Islands.

323. *Abudefduf aureus* (Cuvier). Close up of the head showing the blue pigment in the eye. Photo by Dr. Herbert R. Axelrod. Marau, Br. Solomon Islands.

324. *Abudefduf behni* (Bleeker). Adult stage. The young "bitaeniatus" stage (PMF-1 p. 206) has horizontal black stripes. Photo by Dr. Herbert R. Axelrod. Marau, Br. Solomon Islands.

325. *Cheilinus chlorourus* (Bloch). The dotted Maori wrasse has also gone under the name *Thalliurus chlorourus*. It grows to a length of about 10-12 inches. Photo by Pierre Laboute. New Caledonia.

326. *Cheilinus chlororus* (Bloch). Juvenile. The spotted pattern is emerging and a small bulls-eye can be seen at the base of the tail. Photo by Dr. Herbert R. Axelrod. Marau, Br. Solomon Islands.

327. *Cheilinus undulatus* Ruppell. The size of this fish can be judged by the hatch-cover it is lying on. And yet it is still relatively small compared to the 7 feet it can grow to. Photo by Dr. Herbert R. Axelrod. Marau, Br. Solomon Islands.

328. *Cheilinus undulatus* (Ruppell). A close up of the head showing the large lips (note also the teeth) and red line in the eye. Photo by Dr. Herbert R. Axelrod. Marau, Br. Solomon Islands.

329. *Cheilinus diagrammus* (Lacepede). Juveniles are usually mottled in color with very few distinguishing features. This one has dark marks on its sides. Photo by Dr. Herbert R. Axelrod. Marau, Br. Solomon Islands.

330. *Cheilinus diagrammus* (Lacepede). Larger specimens start to develop the diagonal lines from the eye to the corner of the opercle which are characteristic of this species. Photo by Dr. Herbert R. Axelrod. Marau, Br. Solomon Islands.

331. *Cheilinus diagrammus* (Lacepede). Although red at this stage, larger specimens are greenish. Perhaps we can present a color photo of the adult in a future volume of *Pacific Marine Fishes*. Photo by Dr. Herbert R. Axelrod. Marau, Br. Solomon Islands.

332. *Hemipteronotus taeniourus* (Lacepede). This strange wrasse is a proficient sand-diver. A collector usually has to "dig" one out and net it as it pops out of the sand. Photo by Dr. Gerald R. Allen. Madang, New Guinea.

333. *Cheilinus diagrammus* (Lacepede). At times this species develops light horizontal stripes. It reaches a length of about 1½ feet. Photo by Dr. Gerald R. Allen. Madang, New Guinea.

334. *Pseudodax moluccanus* (Cuvier and Valenciennes). This young indigo wrasse lacks the strong yellow bar at the base of the tail fin as seen in PMF-2 p. 443. Photo by Dr. Herbert R. Axelrod. Marau, Br. Solomon Islands.

335. *Pseudodax moluccanus* (Cuvier and Valenciennes). A cleaner checks the gill area of this wrasse. The bright colors around the mouth draw ones attention to the unusual tooth development of this species. Photo by Allan Power. Santo, New Hebrides.

336. *Paracheilinus filamentosus* Allen. This is a juvenile of the beautiful fish on the opposite page. This species was only recently discovered and named by Dr. Gerald R. Allen. Photo by Dr. Herbert R. Axelrod. Marau, Br. Solomon Islands.

337. An unidentified wrasse (?) makes a hasty departure as the photographer approaches. It didn't quite make it out of the range of the flash. Photo by Dr. Herbert R. Axelrod. Marau, Br. Solomon Islands.

338. *Paracheilinus filamentosus* Allen. A spectacular wrasse that may have escaped detection because of a deep water existence. Photo by Dr. Gerald R. Allen. Guadalcanal, Br. Solomon Islands (75 feet deep).

339. *Thalassoma lutescens* (Lay and Bennett). The bright yellow juvenile shown here is often imported for marine fish fanciers. Photo by Dr. Gerald R. Allen. Madang, New Guinea (20 feet deep).

340. *Thalassoma lunare* (Linnaeus). Adult wrasses are usually quite colorful. The pink and green pattern on this species' head is very attractive. Photo by Dr. Gerald R. Allen of a 5-inch specimen. Madang, New Guinea (20 feet deep).

341. *Thalassoma lutescens* (Lay and Bennett). An adult of the yellow juvenile seen on the opposite page. It may have been captured here by the flash picking at the invertebrates which cover this rocky area. Photo by Allan Power. Santo, New Hebrides.

342. *Halichoeres centiquadrus* (Lacepede). The wide-ranging checkerboard wrasse is found throughout Melanesia. This excellent photo shows its colors very clearly. Photo by Allan Power. Santo, New Hebrides.

343. *Thalassoma hardwicke* (Bennett). This species changes little if any over its broad Indo-Pacific range. The African male (PMF-3, p. 617) looks almost identical to this one from Melanesia. Photo by Dr. Herbert R. Axelrod. Marau, Br. Solomon Islands.

344. *Halichoeres margaritaceus* (Valenciennes). A small wrasse that does not get much over four inches in length. This one is about average size for the species. Photo by Dr. Gerald R. Allen. Madang, New Guinea (26 feet deep).

345. *Epibulus insidiator* (Pallas). A young specimen which has recently lost the white striping of the juvenile (PMF-2, p. 441). Photo by Dr. Herbert R. Axelrod. Marau, Br. Solomon Islands.

346. *Epibulus insidiator* (Pallas). As it grows, the caudal fin takes on a crescentric shape. A fully grown individual may reach over one foot in length. Photo by Dr. Herbert R. Axelrod. Marau, Br. Solomon Islands.

347. *Epibulus insidiator* (Pallas). This fully grown specimen was too large for the photo tank. Aquarists beware! The mouth can really open up wide and engulf small fishes. Choose its tank-mates accordingly. Photo by Dr. Herbert R. Axelrod. Marau, Br. Solomon Islands.

348. *Epibulus insidiator* (Pallas). The telescopefish, as it is sometimes called, may vary in color from yellow to various shades of brown. Photo by Allan Power. Santo, New Hebrides.

349. *Bodianus mesothorax* (Schneider). If the fins are folded like this in an aquarium, it usually means trouble. Here on the reef the fish may just be frightened or accidentally caught in this pose by the photographer's flash. Photo by Dr. Gerald R. Allen. Florida Island, Br. Solomon Islands (30 feet deep).

350. *Bodianus loxozonus* (Snyder). Many different types of coral provide hiding places on the reef. The butterflyfish in the background in front of the wrasse is *Chaetodon pelewensis*. Photo by Pierre Laboute. New Caledonia.

351. *Bodianus diana* (Lacepede). One of the prettier species of *Bodianus*. It grows to a length of about 9 inches. Photo by Dr. Herbert R. Axelrod. Marau, Br. Solomon Islands.

352. *Pseudocheilinus hexataenia* (Bleeker). The six-lined wrasse can usually be found around reefs in relatively shallow water. Photo by Dr. Herbert R. Axelrod. Marau, Br. Solomon Islands.

353. *Pseudocheilinus evanidus* Jordan and Evermann. This wrasse was originally described from Hilo, Hawaii. Photo by Dr. Herbert R. Axelrod. Marau, Br. Solomon Islands.

354. *Wetmorella ocellata* Schultz and Marshall. This species is closely related to *W. philippina*, which has dark spots on the caudal fin. Photo by Dr. Herbert R. Axelrod. Marau, Br. Solomon Islands.

355. *Wetmorella ocellata* Schultz and Marshall. The juvenile (lower fish) has extra white bars on the side but otherwise is very similar to the adult. Photo by Dr. Herbert R. Axelrod. Marau, Br. Solomon Islands.

356. *Labroides dimidiatus* (Cuvier and Valenciennes). Species of *Labroides* do not do well in captivity and usually decline in a week or so. Photo by Dr. Herbert R. Axelrod. Marau, Br. Solomon Islands.

357. A young *Labroides dimidiatus* maintains a cleaning station on the reef where fishes come to be rid of their parasites. Photo by Dr. Herbert R. Axelrod. Marau, Br. Solomon Islands.

358. *Labropsis* sp. Possibly an undescribed species or young form of a known species. Photo of a 3-inch individual by Dr. Gerald R. Allen. Madang, New Guinea (60 feet deep).

359. *Cirrhilabrus solorensis* Bleeker. The long pelvic fin rays help identify this species. Photo by Dr. Herbert R. Axelrod. Marau, Br. Solomon Islands.

360. *Lienardella fasciata* (Gunther). This fish looks a great deal like a parrotfish, but notice the separate teeth characteristic of wrasses. Photo by Allan Power. Santo, New Hebrides.

361. *Cirrhilabrus temmincki* Bleeker. Juveniles have a dark spot on the caudal peduncle at the base of the tail fin. Photo by Dr. Herbert R. Axelrod. Marau, Br. Solomon Islands.

362. *Cirrhilabrus temmincki* Bleeker. As the fish grows the spot becomes smaller and eventually fades. Photo by Dr. Herbert R. Axelrod. Marau, Br. Solomon Islands.

363. *Cirrhilabrus solorensis* Bleeker. The blue of this fish in its natural environment is very evident. In the fish on the opposite page this color may have faded due to fright at being netted and photographed. Photo by Dr. Gerald R. Allen. Madang, New Guinea (25 feet deep).

364. *Scarops rubroviolaceus* (Bleeker). Adult male. Parrotfishes usually get quite large. This one was already too big for the photo tank. Photo by Dr. Herbert R. Axelrod. Marau, Br. Solomon Islands.

365. *Scarops rubroviolaceus* (Bleeker). These strong teeth are used for biting off pieces of coral. Keep your fingers away from them. Photo by Dr. Herbert R. Axelrod. Marau, Br. Solomon Islands.

366. *Scarus troscheli* Bleeker. This species has only been recorded from the western Pacific Ocean. It grows to over one foot in length. Photo by Heiko Bleher. Marau, Br. Solomon Islands.

367. *Scarus troscheli* Bleeker. The white patch on the side of the head makes *S. troscheli* easily recognizable. Photo by Allan Power. Santo, New Hebrides.

368. *Bolbometapon bicolor* (Ruppell). This parrotfish is holding very still as two *Labroides dimidiatus* go over every inch for parasites. Photo by Allan Power. Santo, New Hebrides.

369. *Scarops rubroviolaceus* (Bleeker). At night even parrotfishes take on a color different from the normal daytime pattern. This one is sporting a wide white band. Photo by Dr. Herbert R. Axelrod. Marau, Br. Solomon Islands.

370. *Scarus erythrodon* (Smith). Undisturbed by the diver, this parrotfish nibbles away at a brain coral. Photo by Allan Power. Santo, New Hebrides.

371. *Scarus fasciatus* Valenciennes. This species is called the tattooed parrotfish because of the vermiculations on the head. Photo by Allan Power. Santo, New Hebrides.

372. *Scarus mus* (Smith). The range of *S. mus* is said to be the western Pacific and Indian Oceans. Photo by Allan Power. Santo, New Hebrides.

373. *Diademichthys lineatus* (Sauvage). This species is found closely associated with the sea urchins *Diadema savignyi* or *D. setosum*. Photo by Dr. Herbert R. Axelrod. Marau, Br. Solomon Islands.

374. *Diademichthys lineatus* (Sauvage). The normal color is black, but it turns reddish when preserved (or frightened?). Photo by Dr. Herbert R. Axelrod. Marau, Br. Solomon Islands.

375. *Hoplolatilus* sp. This apparently is a new species, but the specimens were lost and are no longer available. We would like to obtain more specimens. Photo by Dr. Herbert R. Axelrod. Marau, Br. Solomon Islands.

Family BLENNIIDAE
BLENNIES

Blennies are occasionally kept by marine aquarists, not so much for their bright colors (although some species are quite colorful) as for their antics and "personality." Most blennies are bottom dwellers and remain hidden around aquarium decorations or actually live in a tube in the rocks or coral. They are generally very shy and sit near shelter, retiring from sight at the approach of presumed danger. But they do become more tame with time and can be induced to come out for food in a very short time. If you take a very close look at some blennies, you are often in for a treat. From a distance they may look uninteresting and dull, but close up they are appealing and even comical in appearance. The various cirri and fringes, the bluntish head and the large eyes combine to attract one's attention.

But not all blennies are consistent bottom dwellers. There is a whole group of genera which spend some of their time swimming in open water, although not too far from the protection of the reef. These are species generally involved in mimetic relationships with other blennies as well as other fishes. These blennies have been studied by Drs. V.G. Springer and W.F. Smith-Vaniz. They found many things of interest about these fishes during their research, including what appears to be a poison gland at the base of the large canine teeth of the lower jaw in *Meiacanthus*. Fortunately the bite of this fish is not very toxic to humans, as Dr. Smith-Vaniz, who induced one of these fishes to bite him, can attest. He reports there was little pain, but a welt and reddened area appeared which lasted some 14 hours. In the interest of science he repeated the experiment and added a *Plagiotremus* bite for comparison. The *Plagiotremus* bite was no worse than some pin pricks, whereas the *Meiacanthus* bite reacted the same as the first time. Aquarists are therefore warned that they should handle these particular blennies with care but not to be overly concerned if they are bitten, unless symptoms beyond what Dr. Smith-Vaniz experienced occur.

376. *Plagiotremus rhinorhynchos* (Bleeker). This blenny has made use of an old encrusted bottle for its burrow. A substitute burrow may also be constructed out of glass or non-toxic plastic tubes in the aquarium. Photo by Allan Power. Santo, New Hebrides.

377. *Meiacanthus atrodorsalis* (Gunther). This is one of the species involved in mimetic relationships with other blennies. Photo by Dr. Herbert R. Axelrod. Marau, Br. Solomon Islands.

378. *Ecsenius namiyei* (Jordan and Evermann). Species of *Ecsenius* lack a head crest and have none of the caudal fin rays branched. Photo by Dr. Herbert R. Axelrod. Marau, Br. Solomon Islands.

379. *Ecsenius namiyei* (Jordan and Evermann). The same species as above but with some additional color in the caudal area. Photo by Dr. Herbert R. Axelrod. Marau, Br. Solomon Islands.

380. *Meiacanthus* sp. This apparent new species of *Meiacanthus* was discovered by Dr. Gerald R. Allen. Photo of a 3-inch individual by Dr. Gerald R. Allen, Madang, New Guinea.

381. *Meiacanthus atrodorsalis oualanensis* (Gunther). It has been reported that this subspecies of blenny comes only from the Fiji Islands. Photo by Dr. Gerald R. Allen. Suva, Fiji Islands (6 feet deep).

382. *Meiacanthus grammistes* (Valenciennes). Species of this genus appear to have a toxic bite. Handle them with care. Photo by Dr. Herbert R. Axelrod. Marau, Br. Solomon Islands.

383. *Meiacanthus grammistes* (Valenciennes). A reef photo with the blenny in company with several damselfishes and cardinalfishes. Photo by Heiko Bleher. Marau, Br. Solomon Islands.

384. *Plagiotremus rhinorhynchos* (Bleeker). Widely distributed in the western Indian and western Pacific Oceans. Photo by Dr. Herbert R. Axelrod. Marau, Br. Solomon Islands.

385. *Aspidontus taeniatus* Quoy and Gaimard. This Indo-Pacific mimic blenny reaches a length of about five inches. Photo by Dr. Herbert R. Axelrod. Marau, Br. Solomon Islands.

386. *Aspidontus taeniatus* Quoy and Gaimard. Another blenny that has adopted an old bottle as its home. With just the blenny's head visible, the bottle opening should be easily defendable. Photo by Allan Power. Santo, New Hebrides.

387. *Ecsenius* sp., probably *E. yaeyamaensis* (Aoyagi). Worm tubes that are unoccupied offer ready-made burrows for blennies. Some worm tubes in this photo are still occupied. Photo by Heiko Bleher. Marau, Br. Solomon Islands.

388. *Ecsenius yaeyamaensis* (Aoyagi). Blennies often rest on coral or rock with their tails curled in this fashion. The tail might be cocked for a rapid departure. Photo of a 2-inch individual by Dr. Gerald R. Allen. Madang, New Guinea (30 feet deep).

389. *Ecsenius yaeyamaensis* (Aoyagi). The "Y"-shaped mark at the pectoral base is one of the characteristics of this species. Photo by Dr. Herbert R. Axelrod. Marau, Br. Solomon Islands.

390. *Ecsenius collettei* Springer. This species was originally collected at Madang, New Guinea by Dr. Bruce Collette. The species was named in his honor. Photo by Dr. Gerald R. Allen. Madang, New Guinea (10 feet deep).

391. *?Eleotris* sp. Eleotrids are often found in brackish to fresh waters. Photo by Dr. Herbert R. Axelrod. Marau, Br. Solomon Islands.

392. *Ophiocara* sp. There are a great number of different types of gobies. Except for a few, they are difficult to identify. Photo by Dr. Herbert R. Axelrod. Marau, British Solomon Islands.

393. *Eleotris* sp., probably *E. fuscus* (Bloch and Schneider). A brackish or fresh water fish that reaches a length of over 6 inches. Photo by Dr. Herbert R. Axelrod. Marau, Br. Solomon Islands.

394. *Stigmatogobius javanicus* (Bleeker). The first dorsal fin was damaged during capture and what looks like a dark edge to the fin is actually a large black spot. Photo by Dr. Herbert R. Axelrod. Marau, Br. Solomon Islands.

395. *Cryptocentrus fontanesii* (Bleeker). This 5-inch goby is ready to defend its burrow (or retreat into it if need be). Note the united pelvic fins typical of many gobies. Photo by Dr. Gerald R. Allen. Guadalcanal, Br. Solomon Islands (50 feet deep).

396. *Sicyopterus* cf. *longifilis* de Beaufort. Species of the genus *Sicyopterus* are generally found in rivers and estuaries. Photo by Dr. Herbert R. Axelrod. Marau, Br. Solomon Islands.

397. *Oplopomus* sp. Even though somewhat battered, this goby still retains much of its delicate coloration. Photo by Dr. Herbert R. Axelrod. Marau, Br. Solomon Islands.

398. *Amblygobius decussatus* (Bleeker). A small but pretty goby found in the Philippines, East Indies, and Melanesia. It reaches a length of about 3 inches. Photo by Dr. Herbert R. Axelrod. Marau, Br. Solomon Islands.

399. *Petrocheiliops* sp. A strikingly beautiful goby that may be a species new to science. Photo by Dr. Herbert R. Axelrod. Marau, Br. Solomon Islands.

400. *Petrocheiliops* sp. There are many beautiful gobies such as this one, but few are imported for the aquarium trade. They would probably make very good aquarium fishes. Photo by Dr. Herbert R. Axelrod. Marau, Br. Solomon Islands.

401. *Cryptocentrus* sp., probably close to *C. filifer* (Cuvier and Valenciennes). Specimens of this and the other two gobies on this page were lost, so no specific identifications can be given. They may even represent new species. Photo by Dr. Herbert R. Axelrod. Marau, Br. Solomon Islands.

402. *Yongeichthys criniger* (Cuvier and Valenciennes). A marine goby that reaches a length of about 6 inches. Its range covers the western Pacific and Indian Oceans. Photo of a 6-inch individual by Dr. Gerald R. Allen. Guadalcanal, Br. Solomon Islands.

403. *Hypseleotris guentheri* (Bleeker). Known from fresh water streams in New Guinea, and ranges from the East Indies through Melanesia. Photo by Dr. Herbert R. Axelrod. Marau, Br. Solomon Islands.

404. *Amblygobius phalaena* (Cuvier and Valenciennes). Closely related to the Indian Ocean *A. albimaculatus* (see PMF-3, pp. 634-5), but the barred pattern of the body is different and distinctive. Photo by Aaron Norman.

405. *Nemateleotris* sp. For the lovers of the flame goby, *N. magnificus*, here is another species just as beautiful. It is hoped they will be available soon for aquarists. Photo of 3-inch individuals by Dr. Gerald R. Allen. Madang, New Guinea (100 feet deep).

406. *Eleotriodes strigatus* (Broussonet). One of the more common aquarium gobies. It reaches a length of six inches or more. Photo of a 5-inch specimen by Dr. Gerald R. Allen. Malaita, Br. Solomon Islands (20 feet deep).

407. *Brotula multibarbata* Temminck and Schlegel. Juvenile specimen. Known in New Guinea as the barbelled eel-pout. Photo by Dr. Herbert R. Axelrod. Marau, Br. Solomon Islands.

408. *Brotula multibarbata* Temminck and Schlegel. Subadult specimen. This species reaches a length of over two feet. They normally are shy fishes found under rocks and ledges during the daytime. Photo by Dr. Herbert R. Axelrod. Marau, Br. Solomon Islands.

409. *Brotula multibarbata* Temminck and Schlegel. A close up of the head showing the barbels which prompted the specific name. Photo by Dr. Herbert R. Axelrod. Marau, Br. Solomon Islands.

410. *Dinematichthys iluocoeteoides* Bleeker. Some relatives of this fish have reduced eyes or may even be blind. Photo by Dr. Herbert R. Axelrod. Marau, Br. Solomon Islands.

411. *Zanclus canescens* (Linnaeus). Moorish idols are easily collected at night on a reef. This individual almost didn't fit into the photo tank. Photo by Dr. Herbert R. Axelrod. Marau, Br. Solomon Islands.

412. *Zebrasoma scopas* (Cuvier). As these fishes grow the dorsal fins become reduced in height and the common name sailfin tang becomes less applicable. Photo by Dr. Herbert R. Axelrod. Marau, Br. Solomon Islands.

413. *Zebrasoma scopas* (Cuvier). Adult individuals may reach a length of about 8 to 9 inches. The white caudal spine is very noticeable in this photo because of the dark background color. Photo by Allan Power. Santo, New Hebrides.

Family ACANTHURIDAE
SURGEONFISHES

Many of the surgeonfishes that are commonly kept in home aquaria have broad ranges which include Melanesia. One of the favorites of marine hobbyists, *Acanthurus lineatus*, is no exception. Lucky for aquarists there is no great change from juvenile to adult, and small individuals are just as colorful as the larger ones. Like other surgeonfishes, however, they need some vegetable matter in their diet to really do well in captivity. Normally they browse on the algae of the reefs, but unfortunately this food is hard to duplicate or find substitutes for.

Another favorite of aquarists, *Paracanthurus hepatus*, is also common in Melanesia. These surgeonfishes are easily collected if the right gear is available. They generally occur in small schools and will dart into a coral head when frightened. In an aquarium they behave much the same way, and patience is needed to get them swimming about where they can be seen.

Acanthurus pyroferus juveniles have been reported as being a mimic of the lemonpeel angelfish, *Centropyge flavissimus*. Juvenile surgeonfish mimicry does not seem to stop with the lemonpeel but includes other angelfishes (*Centropyge heraldi* and *C. vroliki*) as well and the eastern Indian Ocean *Centropyge eibli* appears to be mimicked by a young surgeonfish in that area. It is difficult to believe that all of these angelfishes are mimicked by a single species of surgeonfish, *Acanthurus pyroferus*, as has been suggested. Some of the angelfishes are sympatric (found in the same area) which would mean that the young of *A. pyroferus* would be mimicking more than one species of angelfish in the same place. This is unlikely. There is probably more than one species of surgeonfish involved. Dr. Shen, who provided many of the photos for our last two books, recently described two new species of surgeonfish in the same group as *A. pyroferus* and *A. chronixis*. All of these species might be involved in the angelfish mimicry.

414. *Ctenochaetus striatus* (Quoy and Gaimard). One of the common names for this fish in New Guinea is the orange-dotted hair-toothed tang. It grows to about one foot in length. Photo by Dr. Herbert R. Axelrod. Marau, Br. Solomon Islands.

415. *Ctenochaetus tominiensis* Randall. As far as known this may be the first time a color photo of this fish has appeared in print anywhere. Photo of a 3-inch individual by Dr. Gerald R. Allen. Guadalcanal, Br. Solomon Islands (30 feet deep).

416. *?Acanthurus pyroferus* Kittlitz. Although similar to the typical young of *A. pyroferus*, this individual has no blue markings. Perhaps it is a form which mimics *Centropyge heraldi* much as *Acanthurus pyroferus* does *C. flavissimus*. Photo of a 3-inch fish by Dr. Gerald R. Allen. Suva, Fiji Islands (6 feet deep).

417. *Acanthurus pyroferus* Kittlitz. Adult with lunate caudal fin and darker body color. Photo by Dr. Herbert R. Axelrod. Marau, Br. Solomon Islands.

418. *Acanthurus chronixis* Randall. Belonging to the same group as *A. pyroferus*, this species seems to mimic *Centropyge vroliki* as a juvenile. Photo of a 3-inch specimen by Dr. Gerald R. Allen. Madang, New Guinea (20 feet deep).

419. *Acanthurus bariene* Lesson. This fish was sleeping under a ledge when photographed. Acanthurids would not rest on the sand like this during the day. Photo by Heiko Bleher. Marau, Br. Solomon Islands.

420. *Acanthurus mata* (Cuvier). It is difficult to see what the small fishes are which elicit the cleaning pose of the acanthurid. They are not *Labroides*. If they are the false cleaners (blennies), this fish will probably be bitten and lose a few scales. Photo by Heiko Bleher. Marau, Br. Solomon Islands.

421. *Acanthurus lineatus* (Linnaeus). A rare photo of a juvenile *A. lineatus*. Although the stripes are present, there are subtle differences in pattern in the head and fins. Photo by Dr. Herbert R. Axelrod. Marau, Br. Solomon Islands.

422. *Acanthurus lineatus* (Linnaeus). The photographer caught this fish at rest in a small cave on the reef at night. Photo by Dr. Herbert R. Axelrod. Marau, Br. Solomon Islands.

423. *Acanthurus lineatus* (Linnaeus). This fish is grazing on the algae-covered rock. Photo by Dr. Gerald R. Allen. Florida Islands, Solomon Islands (10 feet deep).

424. *Acanthurus xanthopterus* Cuvier and Valenciennes. One of the larger species of surgeonfishes, reaching a length of 18 inches or more. Photo by Dr. Herbert R. Axelrod. Marau, Br. Solomon Islands.

425. *Acanthurus gahhm* (Forskal). An adult individual which is identifiable by the black "ear" mark and black around the caudal spine. Photo by Dr. Herbert R. Axelrod. Marau, Br. Solomon Islands.

426. *Naso brevirostris* (Cuvier and Valenciennes). It looks as if this individual has run into some trouble if those are truly scrape marks or scars on its side. Photo by Heiko Bleher. Marau, Br. Solomon Islands.

427. *Paracanthurus hepatus* (Linnaeus). Isolated individuals are not usually seen on the reef like this. Its conspecifics are probably not far away. Photo by Dr. Gerald R. Allen. Madang, New Guinea (20 feet deep).

428. *Paracanthurus hepatus* (Linnaeus). This fish may have been surprised by the flash as it was eating. The mouth is open. Notice the calcareous alga *Halimeda* in the foreground. Photo by Allan Power. Santo, New Hebrides.

429. *Siganus puellus* (Schlegel). A pair of colorful rabbitfishes swimming past coral rock. The fish in the background may be *Naso*. Photo by Allan Power. Santo, New Hebrides.

430. *Siganus oramin* (Bloch and Schneider). This siganid at night has taken on a blotchy appearance and blends well with the sea weeds in which it has taken refuge. Photo by Pierre Laboute. New Caledonia.

431. *Siganus lineatus* (Cuvier and Valenciennes). A whole school of these rabbitfishes makes an impressive sight. The bright yellow spot really catches the eye. Photo by Allan Power. Santo, New Hebrides.

432. *Siganus* sp., possibly *S. doliatus* (Cuvier and Valenciennes). The younger forms have fewer vertical stripes if this is truly the adult of *S. doliatus*. Photo by Pierre Laboute. New Caledonia.

433. A combination of species on the reef: *Acanthurus dussumieri, Gnathodentex aurolineatus, Abudefduf saxatilis*, and a species of *Myripristis*. Photo by Pierre Laboute. New Caledonia.

434. *Paracirrhites forsteri* (Schneider). The freckled hawkfish looks a lot like a grouper waiting to engulf its prey. Photo by Allan Power. Santo, New Hebrides.

435. *Oxycirrhites typus* Bleeker. This long-snouted hawkfish is occasionally imported from the Philippines or Hawaii. Photo by Dr. Herbert R. Axelrod. Marau, Br. Solomon Islands.

436. *Cirrhitichthys oxycephalus* (Bleeker). Juveniles look very much like the adults. A wide ranging Indo-Pacific species very likely to be imported for the aquarium trade. Photo by Dr. Herbert R. Axelrod. Marau, Br. Solomon Islands.

437. *Cyprinocirrhites polyactis* (Bleeker). Although most hawkfishes are strictly bottom fishes this species is a plankton feeder and may swim up off the bottom for food. Note the lunate tail fin. Photo by Dr. Herbert R. Axelrod. Marau, Br. Solomon Islands.

438. *Cirrhitichthys falco* Randall. The holotype of this species, a female 41.8 mm standard length, had eggs up to 0.3 mm in diameter. Photo by Dr. Herbert R. Axelrod. Marau, Br. Solomon Islands.

439. *Cirrhitichthys falco* Randall. The same fish as above but here showing the red-spotted tail. Photo by Dr. Herbert R. Axelrod. Marau, Br. Solomon Islands.

440. *Paracirrhites forsteri* (Schneider). This is probably the most common and widespread of the hawkfishes, extending from Hawaii to the coast of Africa. Photo by Dr. Herbert R. Axelrod. Marau, Br. Solomon Islands.

441. *Cyprinocirrhites polyactis* (Bleeker). It is unusual to see a hawkfish in midwater like this. Photo of a 3-inch specimen by Dr. Gerald R. Allen Madang, New Guinea (20 feet deep).

442. *Cirrhitichthys oxycephalus* (Bleeker). The tufts of the dorsal spines and the separate pectoral rays can easily be seen in this photo. Photo by Dr. Gerald R. Allen. Guadalcanal, Br. Solomon Islands (25 feet deep).

443. *Pterois volitans* (Linnaeus). Some aquarists have been able to keep this species in captivity until it reaches full size, some 12-14 inches. Photo by Dr. Gerald R. Allen of an 8-inch individual from Guadalcanal, Br. Solomon Islands (10 feet deep).

444. *Pterois radiata* (Cuvier and Valenciennes). One of the more colorful lionfishes. The spines really look dangerous, don't they? And they really are. Photo by Allan Power. Santo, New Hebrides.

445. *Pterois volitans* (Linnaeus). Lionfishes, depending on their poisonous spines for protection, do not move away quickly at the approach of a diver and therefore make good subjects for underwater photographers. Photo by Allan Power. Santo, New Hebrides.

446. *?Amblyapistus taenianotus* (Cuvier and Valenciennes). Rouge fish have a large sail-like dorsal fin, possibly making this fish resemble some aspect of its environment and thus less likely to predation. Photo of a 4-inch fish by Dr. Gerald R. Allen. Guadalcanal, Br. Solomon Islands (15 feet deep).

447. *Taenionotus triacanthus* Lacepede. Not only do poisonous fishes sit nicely for pictures, but those relying on protective coloration and shape are easy subjects for the camera-man. Photo by Allan Power. Santo, New Hebrides.

448. *Scorpaenodes hirsutus* (Smith). Scorpionfishes may have brightly colored eyes. This one, as you can see, has a striped pattern. Photo by Dr. Herbert R. Axelrod. Marau, Br. Solomon Islands.

449. *Sebastapistes* sp. Normally scorpionfishes like this one are difficult to see. In shallow water it is entirely possible to step on one, thinking it is a rock. Photo by Allan Power. Santo, New Hebrides.

450. *Scorpaenopsis* sp., possibly *S. cirrhosa* (Thunberg). Scorpaenids do well in aquaria, especially if given live foods (small guppies, etc.) occasionally. The lack of bright colors of most species makes them less desirable as aquarium fishes. Photo by Dr. Herbert R. Axelrod. Marau, Br. Solomon Islands.

451. An unidentified scorpaenid probably belonging to either *Parascorpaena* or *Scorpaenopsis*. The characteristics for identifying scorpionfishes are such that it is very difficult to identify the fishes from photographs. Photo by Allan Power. Santo, New Hebrides.

452. *Sufflamen bursa* (Bloch and Schneider). This triggerfish apparently has found something good to eat and is ignoring the diver. Allan Power. Santo, New Hebrides.

453. *Xanthichthys* sp. Probably the young of *X. ringens* (Linnaeus). The caudal fin pattern closely resembles that of *X. ringens* as figured in PMF-5, p. 1345. Photo by Aaron Norman.

454. *Rhinecanthus aculeatus* (Linnaeus). Triggerfishes do well in captivity, and this species is one of the more popular imports. Photo by Dr. Herbert R. Axelrod. Marau, Br. Solomon Islands.

455. *Melichthys vidua* (Solander). The pink-tailed triggerfish is known as the white-tailed trigger-fish in New Guinea. Both colors are present on the tail. Photo by Dr. Herbert R. Axelrod. Marau, Br. Solomon Islands.

456. *Sufflamen chrysoptera* Schneider. An Indo-Pacific triggerfish that reaches a length of about one foot. Photo by Dr. Herbert R. Axelrod. Marau, Br. Solomon Islands.

457. *Rhinecanthus aculeatus* (Linnaeus). The triggerfish appears to be nibbling at the alga *Dictyota*, but probably is not as algae normally does not constitute part of the triggerfish's diet. Photo by Dr. Herbert R. Axelrod. Marau, Br. Solomon Islands.

458. *Sufflamen chrysoptera* Schneider. This is the same species as the one on the opposite page, but the eye to pectoral fin stripe is different. Photo by Dr. Herbert R. Axelrod. Marau, Br. Solomon Islands.

459. *Sufflamen chrysoptera* Schneider. On the reef the tail fin is folded and the white edging is not so conspicuous, but the yellow stripe stands out like the proverbial sore thumb. Photo by Heiko Bleher. Marau, Br. Solomon Islands.

460. *Balistapus undulatus* (Park). A juvenile has the same general coloration as the adult. Photo by Dr. Herbert R. Axelrod. Marau, Br. Solomon Islands.

461. *Balistapus undulatus* (Park). Another aquarium favorite. The brightly colored undulating lines of this species make it readily identifiable. Photo by Dr. Herbert R. Axelrod. Marau, Br. Solomon Islands.

462. The business end of a triggerfish. The teeth are very strong and are used to crush shellfish. Photo by Dr. Herbert R. Axelrod. Marau, Br. Solomon Islands.

463. *Pervagor melanocephalus* (Bleeker). A young filefish that has not developed the bright adult coloration (see PMF-2, p. 399). Photo by Dr. Herbert R. Axelrod. Marau, Br. Solomon Islands.

464. *Amanses scopas* (Cuvier). Filefish like this one are well able to defend themselves. Note the strong dorsal spine, the strong teeth and the patch of spines on each side of its body. Photo by Allan Power. Santo, New Hebrides.

465. *Alutera scripta* (Forster). At night the color pattern of this scrawled filefish changes to a darker, mottled form. Photo by Heiko Bleher. Marau, Br. Solomon Islands.

466. *Alutera scripta* (Forster). This individual is still blotchy but not as dark as the fish above. Perhaps it has been disturbed and is waking up. Photo by Pierre Laboute. New Caledonia.

467. *Oxymonacanthus longirostris* (Bloch and Schneider). The long-snouted filefish is reported to be one of the more difficult filefishes to keep in captivity. Photo by Dr. Herbert R. Axelrod. Marau, Br. Solomon Islands.

468. *Alutera scripta* (Forster). The more normal daytime color pattern of this species, without the dark blotches. Photo by Pierre Laboute. New Caledonia.

469. *Canthigaster janthinopterus* (Bleeker). Often when the puffers are handled roughly while being photographed they will inflate themselves. This specimen apparently was not that excited. Photo by Dr. Herbert R. Axelrod. Marau, Br. Solomon Islands.

470. *Canthigaster janthinopterus* (Bleeker). Slightly inflated, this fish is losing the dark reticulations around the light spots as the belly expands. Photo by Dr. Herbert R. Axelrod. Marau, Br. Solomon Islands.

471. *Arothron hispidus* (Linnaeus). Puffers look like, and usually are, poor swimmers. When cornered, their only means of defense are their ability to inflate and a set of sharp teeth. Photo by Allan Power. Santo, New Hebrides.

472. *Paraluteres prionurus* (Bleeker). With the dorsal spine folded back it is difficult to decide if this is the puffer or the filefish. The long dorsal and anal fins are typical of filefish, contrasting with the short fins of puffers. Photo by Dr. Gerald R. Allen. Madang, New Guinea (30 feet deep).

473. *Canthigaster bennetti* (Bleeker). Small sharp-nosed puffers usually do well in captivity but are not popular. Photo by Dr. Gerald R. Allen. Madang, New Guinea (20 feet deep).

474. *Arothron immaculatus* (Bloch and Schneider). In New Guinea this species is called the narrow-lined toadfish. We would call it the narrow-lined puffer. The small fishes nearby are all cardinalfishes. Photo by Pierre Laboute. New Caledonia.

475. *Arothron hispidus* (Linnaeus). The night coloration of this species includes dark blotches. The white spots remain 24 hours a day. Photo by Allan Power. Santo, New Hebrides.

476. *Arothron mappa* (Lesson). The scribbled puffer reaches a length of about one foot. Photo by Allan Power. Santo, New Hebrides.

477. *Ostracion tuberculatus* Linnaeus. This fish was discovered over an area where a number of clam shells can be seen. Photo by Pierre Laboute. New Caledonia.

478. *Ostracion cubicus* Linnaeus. Some authors have synonymized this species with *O. tuberculatus*, but they have not given convincing evidence. Note the lack of dark spots on the caudal peduncle. Photo by Heiko Bleher. Marau, Br. Solomon Islands.

479. *Canthigaster compressus* (Proce). This rarely photographed sharp-nosed puffer comes from the East Indies, Philippines and Melanesia. Photo of a 4-inch individual by Dr. Gerald R. Allen. Madang, New Guinea (25 feet deep).

Index

Page numbers in **bold** face refer to illustrations

The following index contains entries for subject matter and illustrations contained in this book and its companion volumes, *Pacific Marine Fishes,* 1-5. Some of the names used in earlier volumes of this series, however, have been revised to reflect an updated or otherwise changed nomenclatural standing; all such names listed in text and index of these volumes are listed in this index but are referenced to show the revised identifications.

A

Abalistes stellaris, **395**, **1344**
Ablennes anastomella, **332**
Ablennes hians, **924**, **926**
Abudefduf, 701
Abudefduf affinis, **1025**
Abudefduf amabilis, **304**
Abudefduf annulatus, **738**
Abudefduf aureus, **305**, **1564**
Abudefduf aureus, **196** (See *Chromis analis*)
Abudefduf behni, **200**, **206**, **1036**, **1564**
Abudefduf bengalensis, **194**
Abudefduf biocellatus, **204**, **732**, **733**
Abudefduf bitaeniatus, **206** (See *Abudefduf behni*)
Abudefduf curacao, **1023**
Abudefduf cyaneus, **190**, **192**, **193**, **197**, **203**, **302**, **1036**
Abudefduf dickii, **730**, **1028**, **1559**
Abudefduf dickii, **201** (See *Abudefduf johnstonianus*)
Abudefduf flavipinnis, **1037**
Abudefduf glaucus, **734**, **1033**
Abudefduf johnstonianus, **201**
Abudefduf lacrymatus, **207**, **731**, **735**, **1029**
Abudefduf leucogaster, **200**, **304**, **1558**
Abudefduf leucopomus, **1032**, **1035**
Abudefduf leucozona, **307**, **1034**, **1035**
Abudefduf melanopus, **203**, **306**, **307**, **1034**
Abudefduf oxyodon, **206**
Abudefduf parasema, **303**
Abudefduf parasema, **203** (See *Abudefduf cyaneus*)
Abudefduf phoenixensis, **307**
Abudefduf rex, **202**, **1031**
Abudefduf saxatilis, **195**, **1023**, **1024**, **1025**, **1617**
Abudefduf septemfasciatus, **1023**
Abudefduf sexfasciatus, **195**, **736**, **1024**
Abudefduf sordidus, **194**, **306**, **727**, **728**, **729**
Abudefduf sparoides, **737**
Abudefduf thoracotaeniatus, **195**
Abudefduf uniocellata, **190**, **192**, **197** (See *Abudefduf cyaneus*)
Abudefduf vaigiensis, **737**
Abudefduf whitleyi, **1561**
Abudefduf xanthonotus, **203** (See *Abudefduf melanopus*)
Abudefduf xanthurus, **200** (See *Abudefduf behni*)
Abudefduf sp., **201** (See *Pomacentrus dorsalis*)
Abudefduf sp., **200** (See *Abudefduf leucogaster*)
Acanthocepola, 931
Acanthocepola indica, **930**, **931**
Acanthochromis polyacanthus, **1558**
Acanthogobius flavimanus, **179**
Acanthopagrus berda, **1314**
ACANTHURIDAE, 84, 793, 1607
Acanthurus, 803
Acanthurus bariene, **1610**
Acanthurus bleekeri, **384**
Acanthurus chronixis, **796**, 1607, **1609**
Acanthurus dussumieri, **385**, **1617**
Acanthurus gahhm, **382**, **796**, **1612**
Acanthurus glaucopareius, 91, **386**
Acanthurus guttatus, **384**
Acanthurus japonicus, **91**, **386**
Acanthurus leucosternon, **85**, **381**, **797**
Acanthurus lineatus, 85, **90**, **387**, **1148**, **1149**, 1607, **1610**, **1611**
Acanthurus mata, **1610**
Acanthurus nigrofuscus, **86**
Acanthurus olivaceous, **86**, **383**
Acanthurus pyroferus, **89**, 1607, **1608**, **1609**
Acanthurus tennenti, **795**
Acanthurus triostegus, **90**, **792**, **793**
Acanthurus xanthopterus, **1612**
Acanthurus sp., **794**
Acentrogobius cauerensis, **635**
Acentrogobius hoshinonis, **178**
Acentrogobius ornatus, **1014**
Acentrogobius sp., **1014**
Adioryx, 230, 231, 689
Adioryx andamanensis, **691**
Adioryx caudimaculatus, **339**, **691**, **1451**, **1458**
Adioryx cornutum, **1457**
Adioryx diadema, **234**, **1061**, **1452**
Adioryx lacteoguttatus, **339**, **693**, **1063**
Adioryx microstomus, **339**
Adioryx rubra, **235**, **1062**
Adioryx spinifer, **234**, **689**, **690**, **692**, **1454**, **1456**
Adioryx spinosissimus, **1061**
Adioryx tiere, **341**
Adioryx tieroides, **1458**
Adioryx violaceus, **1454**, **1455**
Adioryx xantherythrus, 230, **340**
Adioryx sp., **1061**
Aeoliscus, 319
Aeoliscus strigatus, **320**, **321**, **1416**, **1417**
Aesopia, 1099
Aesopia heterorhinos, 1099
Aetobatus narinari, **1076**
Aetomylaeus, 1077
African clown wrasse, **578**
African squirrelfish, **235**
Aholeholes, **236**, 308
Albula vulpes, **1043**
Alectis ciliaris, **1050**
Alectis indica, **426**, **1050**
Alectis major, **1051**
ALEPISAURIDAE, 1257
Alepisaurus borealis, **1256**
Alepisaurus ferox, **1257**
Alfoncino, **548**, 1161
Allard's clownfish, **705**
Alutera monoceros, **125**
Alutera scripta, **122**, **1356**, **1632**, **1633**
ALUTERIDAE, 819
Amanses scopas, **1350**, **1351**, **1631**
AMARSIPIDAE, 1220
Amblyapistus taenianotus, **517**, **962**, **1624**
Amblycirrhitus, 155, 660
Amblycirrhitus bimacula, **1142**
Amblygobius albimaculatus, **634**, **635**
Amblygobius decussatus, **1600**
Amblygobius phalaena, **1602**
Amora, 219
Amphiprion, 181, **287**
Amphiprion akindynos, 288, **292**
Amphiprion allardi, 701, **705**, **708**
Amphiprion biaculeatus, **190**, **301** (= *Premnas biaculeatus*)
Amphiprion chrysopterus, **191**, **296**, **297**, **1019**, **1547**, **1551**
Amphiprion clarkii, **180**, **183**, **185**, **292**, **704**, **708**, **709**, **714**, **715**, **1018**, **1019**, **1547**, **1548**, **1551**
Amphiprion ephippium, **292**
Amphiprion frenatus, **184**, **186**, **187**, **1020**, **1021**
Amphiprion latezonatus, **289**
Amphiprion laticlavius, **183**
Amphiprion melanopus, **293**, **1545**, **1551**, **1552**
Amphiprion nigripes, **561**, **710-14**
Amphiprion ocellaris, **188**, **189**, **298**, **299**, **300**, **301**, **1021**
Amphiprion percula, **188**
Amphiprion perideraion, **182**, **185**, **294**, **295**, **1017**, 1545, **1548**, **1549**, **1550**
Amphiprion polymnus, **183**
Amphiprion sandaracinos, **188**
Amphiprion tricinctus, **290**, **291**
Amphiprion xanthurus, **180**
Amphiprion sp., **706**, **707**
Amphotistius kuhli, **1394**, **1395**
Anago anago, **352**
Anampses caeruleopunctatus, **144**, **145**, **440**, **623**
Anampses cuvieri, **445**
Anampses meleagrides, **442**, **864**
Anampses neoguinaicus, **863**
Anampses rubrocaudatus, **440** (= *Anampses chrysocephalus*)
Anampses twistii, **440**, **863**
Anampses sp., **142** (See *Anampses neoguinaicus*)
Anemonefishes, 181, 289, 701, 1545
Angelfishes, 7, 39, 781
Angel sharks, 1069
Anglerfish, **509**
Anglerfishes, 258
Anguilla, 260
Anguilla japonica, **351**
ANOMALOPIDAE, 1411
Anomalops katoptron, **1411**
ANTENNARIIDAE, 258

Antennarius biocellatus, **828**
Antennarius chironectes, **529**
Antennarius coccineus, **529**
Antennarius hispidus, **528**
Antennarius indicus, **529**
Antennarius nox, 259
Antennarius nummifer, **258, 1365**
Antennarius phymatodes, **530**
Antennarius sanguifluus, 259
Antennarius tridens, 259, **270, 532**
Antennarius sp., **528**
Anthias, 643
Anthias hutchi, **1469, 1471**
Anthias pleurotaenia, **1467, 1468, 1470**
Anthias squammipinnis, **489, 490, 649, 1224**
Anthias sp., **646, 742, 760, 1467**
Anthiinae, 489, 643
Anyperodon, 643
Anyperodon leucogrammicus, **491, 647**
Aphareus, 675
Aphareus flavivultus, 675
Aphareus furcatus, **675**
Aphareus rutilans, **1293**
Apistus carinatus, **533**
Apodes, 260
Apogon, 241, 678
Apogon apogonoides, **463**
Apogon aroubiensis, **1430, 1436**
Apogon aureus, **1447**
Apogon compressus, **1434, 1435**
Apogon cyanosoma, **243, 679, 967, 1434, 1435**
Apogon erythrinus, **463**
Apogon exostigma, **463**
Apogon fasciatus, **460**
Apogon fraenatus, **460, 1439**
Apogon fragilis, **1442**
Apogon fuscus, **461**
Apogon hartzfeldi, **1437**
Apogon kallopterus, **1438**
Apogon leptacanthus, **460, 1443**
Apogon lineatus, **968**
Apogon nematopterus, **243, 464-465**
Apogon niger, **967**
Apogon novemfasciatus, **242, 969**
Apogon nubilis, **679**, 686
Apogon orbicularis, **243** (See *Apogon nematopterus*)
Apogon robustus, **242**
Apogon savayensis, **678, 1446**
Apogon sealei, **1439**
Apogon semilineatus, **240, 462**
Apogon snyderi, 686
Apogon taeniophorus, **1436**
Apogon taeniopterus, **461**
Apogon trimaculatus, **968**
Apogon uninotatus, 241
Apogon sp., **1437, 1440**
Apogonichthyoides, 678
Apogonichthyoides taeniatus, 685
APOGONIDAE, 241, 678, 1432
Apolemichthys, 786
Apolemichthys arcuatus, **364**
Apolemichthys trimaculatus, **364, 785, 1126, 1127, 1128, 1533**
Apolemichthys xanthurus, **784, 785**
Aprion virescens, **1293**
Arabian pike-eel, **351**
Aracana aurita, **1363**
Archamia, 678
Archamia biguttata, **1445**
Archamia fucata, **682**, 686, **1444, 1445, 1446**
Archamia leai, **1441**
Archamia zosterophora, **1442**
Archamia sp., **1440**
Archerfishes, 327
Arctoscopus japonicus, **273**
Argus-wrasse, **455**
Argyrops spinifer, **1312**
Argyrosomus argentatus, **1321**
Argyrosomus japonicus, **1320**
Argyrosomus nibea, **1320**
Armorheads, 1217
Arnoglossus, 262
Arothron, 97
Arothron aerostaticus, **104**
Arothron alboreticulatus, **105**
Arothron citrinellus, **112, 403**
Arothron hispidus, **106, 107, 109, 113, 409, 1634, 1636**
Arothron immaculatus, **1636**
Arothron mappa, **1637**
Arothron meleagris, **112**
Arothron nigropunctatus, **104, 403, 404**
Arothron niphobles, **113**, 408
Arothron pardalis, **108**
Arothron reticularis, **407**
Arothron rubripes, **406**
Arothron stellatus, **190, 1357**
Arothron stictonotus, **405**
Arothron vermicularis, **409**
Arothron sp., **404**
Aspasmichthys ciconae, **165, 1009**
Aspidontus taeniatus, 159, **471, 1333, 1595**
Assasi triggerfish, **125** (See black-bellied triggerfish)
Astrapogon, 241
Astroconger myriaster, **275**
ATHERINIDAE, 1412
Aulacocephalus temmincki, 252, **495**
AULOPODIDAE, 913
Aulopus japonicus, **914**
Aulopus purpurissatus, **914**
AULOSTOMIDAE, 773
Aulostomus chinensis, **772, 773, 1423**
Auxis thazard, **1328**

B

Balistapus, 815
Balistapus undulatus, **119, 124, 646, 818, 819, 1349, 1630**
Balistes flavimarginatus, **1342, 1343**
BALISTIDAE, 114, 815
Balistoides niger, 114, **115, 116, 123, 396, 814, 815, 1111, 1340-1342**
Balistoides viridescens, **393, 396, 817**
Band-fishes, 931
Banded catshark, **502**
Banded cheilinus, **446, 569**
Banded pipefish, **325**
Banded-tailed goatfish, **344**
Banded wrasse, **144, 582**
Bar-chested damselfish, **195**
Barhead spinefoot, **93, 94**
Barracuda, **698**
Barracudas, 925
Barred jack, **424**
Barred morwong, **247, 481**
Barred perch, **166**
Barred squirrelfish, **234**
Batfishes, 78, 525, 1138
Bathygobius fuscus, **174, 1014, 1015**
Beaked butterflyfish, **73**
Bearded goby, **178**
Beardfishes, 1173
Bellowsfish, 319, **322**
BELONIDAE, 329
Bembras japonicus, **1007**
Bengal devil, **194**
Bennett's butterflyfish, **48, 64, 748**
Bennett's sharpnosed puffer, **402**
Berry frogfish, **529**
BERYCIDAE, 1161
Beryx decadactylus, **549**, 1161
Beryx splendens, **48, 1160**, 1161
Bicolor cleaner wrasse, **136, 593**
Bicolored parrotfish, **154, 458**
Bigeye sea-bream, **435**
Bigeye squirrelfish, **232**
Bigeyes, 231, 551
Big-spine squirrelfish, **233**
Big-teeth cardinalfish, **461**
Bi-ocellated wrasse, **454**
Bird wrasse, 129, **142, 143, 586, 852**
Black-and-white snapper, **288**
Black-and-white striped blenny, **164**
Black-backed butterflyfish, **42, 377**
Black-bar devil, **201**
Black-bellied triggerfish, **125**
Black-belt wrasse, **131, 443**
Black-edge angelfish, **17**
Blackfin gurnard, **536**
Black-finned anemonefish, **714**
Blackfinned triggerfish, **397**
Black-finned triple-spine, **391**
Blackfish, **546**
Black porgy, **237, 438**
Black ribbon eel, **275**
Blackspot goatfish, **343**
Blackspot tuskfish, **859**
Black-spotted puffer, **104, 403**
Black-tailed damselfish, **204**
Blacktip soldierfish, **233, 340**
Black-velvet angelfish, **362**
Blanquillos, 531
Bleeker's surgeonfish, **384**
Blennies, 159, 636, 1591
BLENNIIDAE, 159, 636, 1591
Blennius yatabei, **168**
Blind goby, **478**

Blotched filefish, **126**
Blue-and-gold striped snapper, 227
Blue-and-yellow angelfish, **17**
Blue-and-yellow rock cod, **494**
Bluebacked puffer, **405**
Blue chromis, **190**
Blue-faced angelfish, **30**, **31**, **359**, **783**
Blue-faced blenny, **169**
Blue-finned triggerfish, **393**
Bluefish, **1266**
Blue-girdled angelfish, **28**, **29**, **360**, **361**
Blue gudgeon, **477**
Blue-line goby, **171**
Blue-line pipefish, **325**
Blue-lined angelfish, **32**, **34**, **35**
Blue-lined grouper, **492**
Blue-lined snapper, **227**
Blue reef-fish, **190**, **197**
Blue ribbon eel, **275**, **350**
Blue-ringed angelfish, **26**, **367**
Blue-spotted goby, **178**
Blue-spotted porgy, **437**
Blue-spotted ray, **509**
Blue-spotted snapper, **435**
Blue-spotted wrasse, **144**
Blue-streak devil, **206**
Blue-streak weever, **473**
Bluestripe butterflyfish, **374**
Blue-striped snapper, 221
Blue tang, **87**, **381**
Frontispiece (Book II), **1148**
Blue-trim parrotfish, **154**
Blue whiting, **135**, **531**
Blushing cardinalfish, **463**
Blushing wrasse, **137**
Boarfishes, 1217
Bodianus, 577, 587
Bodianus axillaris, **442**, 577, **590**, **591**, **854**, **855**
Bodianus bilunulatus, **143**, **445**, **856**
Bodianus diana, **131**, 587, **591**, **854**, **858**, **1579**
Bodianus hirsutus, **856**
Bodianus loxozonus, **1578**
Bodianus luteopunctatus, 588, 589
Bodianus mesothorax, **131**, **443**, **854**, **858**, **1578**
Bodianus oxycephalus, **130**, **133**, **879**
Bodianus perdito, 857, **858**
Bodianus sp., **442**, **444**
Bolbometapon bicolor, **154**, **458**, **984**, **985**, **1586**
Boleophthalmus, 172
Bombay ducks, 913
BOTHIDAE, 262
Bothus, 262
Bothus sp., **1095**
Boxfishes, 114
Brachirus biocellatus, **524**, **945**, **946**, **947**
Brama brama, 1171, 1173
Brama japonica, 1171, 1172, 1173
Brama sp., **1170**
BRAMIDAE, 1170
BRANCHIOSTEGIDAE, 531
Branchiostegus argentatus, **533**
Branchiostegus japonicus, **532**
Bream, **437**
Bristle-tail filefish, **400**
Brotula multibarbata, **1604**
Brotulids, 997
Brown angelfish, **35**
Brown-banded angelfish, **364**
Brown-eared surgeonfish, **382**
Brown flathead, **539**
Brownspot cardinalfish, 241
Brownstripe wrasse, **130**
Brown-striped blenny, **164**
Bullseyes, 1254
Butterfish, **417**
Butterfishes, 416, 1220
Butterfly-bream, 666, 1493
Butterflyfin lionfish, **512**, **514**
Butterflyfishes, 39, 743
Butterflymudskipper, **177**

C

Caesio, 221, 673, **742**
Caesio caerulaureus, **677**, **1296**
Caesio chrysozonus, **223**, **1503**
Caesio cuning, **1502**
Caesio pisang, **1503**
Caesio pulcherrimus, **1505**
Caesio xanthonotus, **676**, **1294**
CALLIONYMIDAE, 219
Callionymus, 219
Callionymus picturatus, 220
Callionymus richardsoni, **486**
Callionymus splendidus, 220
Calliurichthys japonicus, **1330**
Calloplesiops altivelis, 156, **244**, **1253**
Callyodon improvisus, **630**
Calotomus japonicus, **995**
Calotomus spinidens, **631**
Canary forktail blenny, **470**
Cantherhines dumerili, **1348**
Cantherhines fronticinctus, **822**
Cantherhines sandwichensis, **1354**, **1355**
Canthidermis maculatus, **120**, **1348**
Canthigaster, 823
Canthigaster bennetti, **402**, **826**, **827**, **1360**, **1635**
Canthigaster cinctus, **110**, **111**, **1359**
Canthigaster compressus, **1638**
Canthigaster jactator, **402**
Canthigaster janthinopterus, **823**, **1361**, **1634**
Canthigaster rivulatus, **98**
Canthigaster solandri, **98**, **402**
Canthigaster valentini, **401**, **825**, **1358**, **1359**
CANTHIGASTERIDAE, 96, 823
Caprodon longimanus, **496**
Caprodon schlegeli, **496**
CARACANTHIDAE, 641
Caracanthus maculatus, **641**
CARANGIDAE, 423
Caranx armatus, **1055**
Caranx bucculentus, **1054**
Caranx delicatissimus, **431**
Caranx helvolus, **430**
Caranx malabaricus, **1053**
Caranx sp., **431**, **1055**
CARAPIDAE, 510
Carapus sp., **510**
CARCHARHINIDAE, 1087
Carcharodon carcharias, **1088**
Cardinalfishes, 240, 678, 1433
Catsharks, 501, 1399
CENTRISCIDAE, 222, 319
Centriscus, 319
CENTROLOPHIDAE, 1220
Centrolophus, 1220
Centropholis petersi, **1171**
Centropyge, 7, 15, 21, 781
Centropyge acanthops, **780**
Centropyge bicolor, **26**, **1133**, **1540**, **1541**
Centropyge bispinosus, **27**, **365**, **781**, **1133**
Centropyge ferrugatus, frontispiece, **20**, **21**, **1129**, **1130**
Centropyge fisheri, **365**
Centropyge flavissimus, 8, 18, **20**, **363**, **781**, **1543**, 1607
Centropyge heraldi, **8**, **18**, **19**, **1131**, 1607
Centropyge loriculus, **22**, **23**, **24**, 781
Centropyge multifasciatus, **1542**
Centropyge multispinus, **782**
Centropyge nox, **362**, **1134**
Centropyge potteri, **363**
Centropyge tibicen, **25**, **363**, **1134**, **1135**
Centropyge vroliki, **20**, 85, **365**, **1132**, **1542**, 1607
Centropyge sp., **37**
Cephalopholis, 252, 643
Cephalopholis argus, **499**, **642**, **1237**
Cephalopholis aurantius, **1238**, **1484**, **1486**
Cephalopholis boenack, **492**, **644**, **1236**
Cephalopholis coatesi, **1483**
Cephalopholis leopardus, **652**, **1486**
Cephalopholis miniatus, **491**, **492**, **1485**, **1487**
Cephalopholis pachycentron, **1237**, **1489**
Cephalopholis rogaa, **646**
Cephalopholis urodelus, **500**, **1239**, **1485**
CEPOLIDAE, 931
Cepola, 931
Ceram wrasse, **147**
Chaenogobius urotaenia, **478**
Chaetoderma pencilligera, **398** (See *Chaetodermis spinosissimus*)
Chaetodermis spinosissimus, **398**, **1352**, **1358**
Chaetodipterus, 1139
Chaetodon, 761
Chaetodon adiergastos, **57**, **1191**

Chaetodon argentatus, 65, 1194
Chaetodon aureus, 40
Chaetodon auriga, 54, 55, 749, 1205
Chaetodon baronessa, 1192, 1525
Chaetodon bennetti, 48, 64, 379, 748, 1187
Chaetodon "chrysurus," 750, 751
Chaetodon citrinellus, 72, 376, 755, 1198, 1199
Chaetodon daedalma, 53
Chaetodon ephippium, 44, 46, 47, 49, 375, 1179, 1520, 1521
Chaetodon falcula, 52, 759, 760, 761, 765
Chaetodon flavirostris, 1520, 1524, 1547
Chaetodon fremblii, 374
Chaetodon guentheri, 65, 1199
Chaetodon guttatissimus, 752, 753
Chaetodon kleini, 41, 374, 743, 744, 745, 1196, 1197, 1520, 1522, 1523
Chaetodon lineolatus, 42, 379, 764, 765, 1192, 1193
Chaetodon lunula, 50, 51, 1188
Chaetodon melannotus, 42, 377, 752, 1182
Chaetodon mertensi, 45, 63
Chaetodon meyeri, 65, 756, 757, 758
Chaetodon miliaris, 374
Chaetodon modestus, 62, 1196
Chaetodon multicinctus, 48
Chaetodon nippon, 49, 66
Chaetodon octofasciatus, 66, 372, 1186, 1187
Chaetodon ornatissimus, 59, 64, 1181, 1520, 1521
Chaetodon pelewensis, 1520
Chaetodon pictus, 763
Chaetodon plebeius, 64, 373, 379, 762, 1180, 1181
Chaetodon punctatofasciatus, 53, 1195, 1520
Chaetodon quadrimaculatus, 50
Chaetodon rafflesi, 52, 1200, 1201
Chaetodon reticulatus, 43, 377, 1200
Chaetodon semeion, 63, 754, 1183
Chaetodon speculum, 41, 43, 373, 1191
Chaetodon strigangulus, 67
Chaetodon tinkeri, 378
Chaetodon triangulum, 57, 58, 378, 379, 743
Chaetodon trifascialis, 45, 67, 380, 1202, 1524
Chaetodon trifasciatus, 55, 60-61, 755, 1203, 1526, 1527
Chaetodon ulietensis, 1204, 1205, 1528
Chaetodon unimaculatus, 43, 1190, 1524
Chaetodon vagabundus, 56, 376, 1188, 1520, 1527
Chaetodon wiebeli, 67, 1185
Chaetodon xanthocephalus, 743, 746, 747
Chaetodon xanthurus, 63, 1184
CHAETODONTIDAE, 39, 743, 1520
Chaetodontoplus, 781
Chaetodontoplus chrysocephalus, 8, 35
Chaetodontoplus duboulayi, 1121
Chaetodontoplus melanosoma, 8, 35, 362, 1123
Chaetodontoplus mesoleucus, 36, 37
Chaetodontoplus personifer, 1121, 1122, 1123
Chaetodontoplus septentrionalis, 8, 32, 33, 34, 1119, 1120
CHANIDAE, 1044
Chanos chanos, 1044
Chasmichthys dolichognathus, 178
Chasmichthys gulosus, 178, 478
Chaunax fimbriatus, 525, 1094
Checkerboard wrasse, 147, 454, 455, 605
Cheilinus, 128, 569
Cheilinus bimaculatus, 573, 894
Cheilinus ceramensis, 147
Cheilinus chlorourus, 896, 1565, 1566
Cheilinus diagrammus, 1567, 1568
Cheilinus fasciatus, 446, 569-571 •
Cheilinus oxycephalus, 894, 895
Cheilinus rhodochrous, 895
Cheilinus trilobatus, 572, 896, 898
Cheilinus undulatus, 441, 574, 1566
Cheilio inermis, 447, 592, 872, 873
CHEILODACTYLIDAE, 251
Cheilodactylus, 251
Cheilodipterus, 678, 1432
Cheilodipterus lachneri, 681, 686
Cheilodipterus lineatus, 680, 681
Cheilodipterus macrodon, 461, 966, 1432, 1433
Cheilodipterus quinquelineatus, 1433
Cheilodipterus zonatus, 1437
Cheilodipterus sp., 1430
Chelidonichthys kumu, 537
Chelidoperca hirundinacea, 1226
Chelmon, 761
Chelmon rostratus, 38, 73, 371, 761
Chevron butterflyfish, 45
Chilomycterus, 96
Chiloscyllium colax, 502
Chiloscyllium griseum, 1082
Chiloscyllium indicum, 1083
Chimaera phantasma, 1080
Chinese mudskipper, 177
Chinese sergeant-major, 195
Choerodon azurio, 150, 451, 860
Choerodon schoenleinii, 133, 859, 860
Choerodon sp., 133, 149
Chorinemus orientalis, 1056, 1057
Chorinemus tolooparah, 1057
Chromis, 717
Chromis amboinensis, 1554
Chromis analis, 196, 1553
Chromis atripectoralis, 190, 1040
Chromis atripes, 1556
Chromis caeruleus, 190 (See Chromis atripectoralis)
Chromis caeruleus, 1040
Chromis dimidiatus, 207, 218
Chromis lineatus, 1556
Chromis lepidolepis, 1556
Chromis margaritifer, 1039, 1554
Chromis notatus, 207, 306, 1038
Chromis richardsoni, 1039
Chromis rollandi, 1557
Chromis ternatensis, 718
Chromis xanthochir, 1038
Chromis xanthurus, 1557
Chromis sp., 700, 1561, 1563
Chrysophrys auratus, 1316
Chrysophrys major, 434, 437
Cigar wrasse, 447, 592, 872
Cinnamon flounder, 276
Cirrhilabrus exquisitus, 581, 870
Cirrhilabrus solorensis, 870, 1582, 1583
Cirrhilabrus temmincki, 1582
Cirrhilabrus sp., 871
Cirrhitichthys, 660
Cirrhitichthys aprinus, 157, 488
Cirrhitichthys aureus, 158, 487
Cirrhitichthys falco, 1143, 1620
Cirrhitichthys oxycephalus, 158, 1619, 1621
CIRRHITIDAE, 155, 660, 1113
Cirrhitops, 663
Cirrhitus pinnulatus, 1142, 1144
Cirripectes, 636
Cirripectes variolosus, 637
Cirripectes sp., 1336, 1337
Citron butterflyfish, 72, 376
Citron goby, 479
Cleaner wrasse, 39, 129, 159, 453, 1569
Clingfishes, 1009
CLINIDAE, 159, 636
Clown anemonefish, 188
Clownfish, 188
Clown surgeonfish, 387
Clown sweetlips, 225, 345, 346
Clown triggerfish, 114, 115, 116, 123, 396, 814
Clown wrasse, 140, 448, 576, 849
Clupea pallasi, 315, 317
CLUPEIDAE, 313
Cobia, 1321, 1322
Cockatiel wrasse, 892
Cold porgy, 139
Cololabias saira, 331
Comet, 244, 1253
Comet grouper, 261
Conger eels, 260, 1399
Conger japonicus, 352
CONGRIDAE, 260, 1399
CONGROGADIDAE, 638
Convict surgeonfish, 793
Convict tang, 90
Convict worm-goby, 420
Copperband butterflyfish, 371
Coradion altivelis, 1525
Coradion chrysozonus, 380

Coradion fulvocinctus, **62**
Coral beauty, **27**, **365**
Coral hogfish, **442**, **590**, **591**
Coral parrotfish, **458**
Coral spinefoot, **390**
Coreoperca kawamebari, **522**, **1235**
Coris, 569
Coris africana, **576**, **578**
Coris aygula, **141**, **575**, **850**, **851**
Coris caudimacula, **580**
Coris flavovittata, **448**
Coris formosa, **578**, **579**
Coris gaimard, **140**, **448**, **576**, **579**, **848**, **849**
Coris rosea, **448**
Coris variegata, **441**
Coris venusta, **848**
Coris yamashiroi, **137**
Corniger, 230
Coromandel grouper, **250**, **253**
Coryphaena equiselis, 1260
Coryphaena hippurus, 1260, **1261**
CORYPHAENIDAE, 1261
Corythoichthys intestinalis, **699**
Cottogobius yongei, **476**
Croakers, 1319
Cromileptes, 643
Cromileptes altivelis, 252, **256**, **527**
Crosshatch butterflyfish, **63**
Crosshatch triggerfish, **118**
Crowned blenny, **163**, **471**
Crowned sea horse, **212**
Cryptocentrus sp., **1601**
Cryptocentrus filifer, **1601**
Cryptocentrus fontanesii, **1599**
Cryptocentrus sp., **1601**
Ctenochaetus, 803
Ctenochaetus cyanoguttatus, **801**, **1155**
Ctenochaetus striatus, **802**, **803**, **1607**
Ctenochaetus strigosus, **387**, **801**, **1147**
Ctenochaetus tominiensis, **1608**
Ctenoscolopsis, 1493
Ctenoscolopsis ciliatus, **1493**, **1494**
Ctenotrypauchen microcephalus, **478**
Cusk-eels, 997
Cutlassfishes, 927
Cuvier's wrasse, **445**
Cynoscion macdonaldi, 1319
Cypselurus opisthopus, **330**
Cypselurus pinnatibarbatus, **992**
Cypselurus poecilopterus, **922**
Cyprinocirrhites, 663, 1143
Cyprinocirrhites polyactis, **1619**, **1621**

D

DACTYLOPTERIDAE, 534
Dactylopterus orientalis, **534**
Dactylopus, 219
Daicocus peterseni, **535**, **963**
Dampierosa, 959
Damselfishes, 181, 289, 701, 1545
Dascyllus, 181, 289, 290, 701
Dascyllus albisella, **303**
Dascyllus aruanus, **202**, **702**, **738**, **1022**
Dascyllus carneus, 701, **703**
Dascyllus marginatus, **198-199**
Dascyllus melanurus, **204**, **1553**
Dascyllus reticulatus, **205**, 701, **703**, **1022**
Dascyllus trimaculatus, **205**, **303**, **714**, **1553**
Dascyllus sp., **661**, **700**
Dash-dot cardinalfish, **463**
Dasson trossulus, **164**
(See *Petroscirtes breviceps*)
DASYATIDAE, 509, 1393
Dasyatis akajei, **509**
Dasyatis gerrardi, **1078**
Datnioides, 1265
Decapterus, 423
Decapterus russellii, **1058**
Decorated triggerfish, **117**, **394**
Dendrochirus, 258, 653
Dendrochirus brachypterus, **524**, **653**
Dendrochirus zebra, **514**, **659**
Dendrochirus zebra, **265**
(See *Pterois antennata*)
Dendrochirus sp., **265**
Devil stinger, **515**, **536**
Diademichthys, 1009
Diademichthys lineatus, **1590**
Diagram sweetlips, **224**
Diana wrasse, **131**
Diaphanous boxfish, **415**
Dictyosoma burgeri, **170**
Dinematichthys, 997
Dinematichthys iluocoeteoides, **996**, **1605**
Diodon, 96
Diodon holacanthus, **103**
Diodon hystrix, 96, **410**, **411**
DIODONTIDAE, 96
Diplogrammus, 219
Diploprion bifasciatum, 252, 489, **492**, **1228**, **1229**
Diproctacanthus xanthurus, **447**
Ditrema temmincki, 335, **336**, **337**
Doderleina berycoides, **1230**
Dolphins, 1261
Doryrhamphus melanopleura, **213**, **325**, 1420
Dotted butterflyfish, **63**
Dottybacks, 156
Double-ocellated scorpionfish, **524**
Double-saddle butterflyfish, **52**
Draculo, 219
Dragon fish, **218**
Dragonets, 219
Drepane, 1141
Drepane longimana, **1140**
Drepane punctata, **1141**
DREPANIDAE, 1138
Drepaninae, 1139
Drums, 1319
Dunckerocampus caulleryi, 1420
Dunckerocampus dactyliophorus, **325**, **1420**, **1421**
Dusky goby, **174**, **478**
Dusky spinefoot, **388**

E

Eagle rays, 1074
Echidna nebulosa, **353**, **1002**, **1403**
Echidna zebra, **354**, 1403
Ecsenius, 636
Ecsenius collettei, **1597**
Ecsenius lineatus, **1336**
Ecsenius namiyei, **1592**
Ecsenius pulcher, **470**
Ecsenius yaeyamaensis, **1596**, **1597**
Ecsenius sp., **1596**
Eight-banded butterflyfish, **66**, **372**
Eight-lined wrasse, **449**
Electric rays, 1067
Elegatis bipinnulatus, **1056**
ELEOTRIDAE, 172, 633
Eleotriodes, 633
Eleotriodes elapoides, **175**, **474**
Eleotriodes strigatus, **474**, **476**, **632**, **633**, **1016**, **1603**
Eleotriodes virgata, **171**
Eleotris fuscus, **1598**
Eleotris sp., **1598**
Eleutherochir, 219
Eleutheronema tetradactylum, **1175**
Elops machnata, **1042**
EMBIOTOCIDAE, 335
Emerald bass, **495**
Emperor angelfish, **8**, **9**, **10**, **11**, **12**, **13**, **688**, **787**
Emperor bream, 663
Emperor snapper, 221, **674**
Engraulis japonica, **1045**
Entomacrodus, 636
Eopsetta grigorjewi, **276**, **542**
EPHIPPIDAE, 1138
Ephippinae, 1138, 1139
Ephippus, 1139
Ephippus orbis, **1139**
Epibulus insidiator, **441**, **887**, **1576**, **1577**
Epinephelus, 643, 652
Epinephelus akaara, **1242**
Epinephelus amblycephalus, **1246**
Epinephelus awoara, **1240**
Epinephelus caeruleopunctatus, **497**, **1246**, **1247**
Epinephelus cometae, **261**, **1243**
Epinephelus coromandelicus, **250**, **253**
Epinephelus damelii, 252
Epinephelus episticus, **1243**
Epinephelus fario, **254**, **645**, **1242**, **1249**, **1251**, **1488**
Epinephelus fasciatomaculatus, **1240**, **1241**
Epinephelus fasciatus, **643**, **500**, **1238**, **1239**, **1250**, **1490**
Epinephelus flavocaeruleus, **494**
Epinephelus hexagonatus, **493**, **1248**

Epinephelus kohleri, **261**
Epinephelus macrospilus, **1247**
Epinephelus megachir, **1249, 1250**
Epinephelus merra, **261, 493, 645, 1244, 1491**
Epinephelus moara, 252, **255, 1242**
Epinephelus rhyncholepis, **1241**
Epinephelus septemfasciatus, **498, 1243**
Epinephelus summana, **497**
Epinephelus tauvina, **493, 1244, 1245**
Epinephelus sp., **254, 1244**
Equetus, 1319
Equula, 1165
Erosa, 959
Erosa erosa, **961**
Escolars, 927
Etelis carbunculus, **1292**
Etrumeus micropus, **1045**
Euthynnus affinis, **1325, 1327**
Euthynnus pelamis, **1325, 1329**
Euxiphipops, 786
Euxiphipops navarchus, **28, 29, 360, 361, 1534**
Euxiphipops sexstriatus, **16, 361, 1124**
Euxiphipops xanthometapon, **30, 31, 359, 783, 1535, 1539**
Eviota abax, **174**
Evistias acutirostris, 1217
Evynnis cardinalis, **1313**
Evynnis japonica, **1313, 1315**
Exallias, 636
Exallias brevis, 640
EXOCOETIDAE, 328, 925

F

False cleaner, **471**
Fan bellied filefish, **400**
Fan-finned frogfish, **529**
Fanfishes, 1170, 1172
Fantailed filefish, **397**
Filament butterflyfish, **54, 55**
Filefishes, 122, 819, 1351
Firefish, **176**
Fisher's angelfish, **365**
Fishing frog, **528**
Fistularia petimba, **324**
Five-lined cardinalfish, **240**
Five-lined goby, **173, 479**
Flag-tailed rock cod, **500**
Flagtail, **791**
Flagtails, 308
Flaming angelfish, **22-23, 24**
Flammeo, 230, 231, 689
Flammeo laeve, **693**
Flammeo operculare, **1452, 1453**
Flammeo sammara, 233, **1452**
Flathead, 538, **775**
Flyingfish, **330, 427**
Flyingfishes, 328, 925
Flying gurnards, 534
Forcipiger, 743
Forcipiger flavissimus, 68, **370**, 743, **770, 1215, 1530**
Forcipiger longirostris, 743
Forktail blenny, **163**
Formio, 1169
Formio niger, **1169**
FORMIONIDAE, 1169
Four-lined wrasse, **449**
Four-spot butterflyfish, **50**
Fowleria, 678
Fowleria aurita, **684**
Foxface, **92**
Fox jacopever, **520**
Franzia fasciatus, **239**
Freckled hawkfish, **157**

G

Galeocerdo cuvieri, 1087
Gaterin, 222
Gaterin albovittatus, **348, 1267, 1268**
Gaterin chaetodonoides, **89, 225, 228, 345, 346, 1269, 1506, 1507, 1509**
Gaterin cinctus, **349**
Gaterin diagrammus, **224**
Gaterin flavomaculatus, **1269**
Gaterin gaterinus, **670**
Gaterin goldmanni, **1511**
Gaterin orientalis, **347, 669, 671, 1271, 1272, 1274, 1275, 1506, 1508, 1510**
Gaterin picus, **228, 1273, 1274, 1511**
Gaterin punctatissimus, **670**
Gaterin sp., **1270**
Gazza, 1165
GEMPYLIDAE, 927
Gempylus serpens, **929**
Genicanthus, 7
Genicanthus fucosus, **17**
Genicanthus lamarck, **12, 19, 1544**
Genicanthus melanospilus, **1544**
Genicanthus semifasciatus, **19**
Genicanthus watanabei, **7, 17, 1128**
Gephyroberyx japonicus, **1161**
Gerres abbreviatus, **919**
Gerres baconensis, **918**
Gerres filamentosus, **917, 920**
Gerres oyena, **771**
GERRIDAE, 917
Ghost butterfish, **419**
Ghost pipefish, **216, 217**
Ghost pipefishes, 214
Giant wrasse, **441, 574**
Girdled sweetlips, **349**
Girella, 433
Girella punctatus, 433, **546**
Girella tricuspidata, 433
Glassfishes, **1430**
Glaucosoma fauveli, 1254, **1255**
Glaucosoma hebraicum, 1255
Glaucosoma magnificus, **1254**
Glaucosoma scapulare, 1161, 1255
GLAUCOSOMIDAE, 1254
Gnathagnus elongatus, **982**
Gnathanodon speciosus, **424, 425, 1052**
Gnathodentex, 666
Gnathodentex aurolineatus, **232, 666, 667, 1500, 1617**
Goatfishes, 259, 739, 1461
Gobies, 172, **633**
GOBIESOCIDAE, 1009
Gobiesox, 1009
GOBIIDAE, 172, 633
Gobiodon, 172
Gobiodon citrinus, **479, 632, 1010**
Gobiodon quinquestrigatus, **173, 479**
Goggle-eye scad, **552**
Gold-bar snapper, **436**
Gold eye-band cardinalfish, **463**
Gold-striped butterfly bream, **439**
Gold-striped cardinalfish, **243**
Golden-banded goatfish, **342**
Golden butterflyfish, **40, 754**
Golden clingfish, **165**
Golden frogfish, **528**
Golden hawkfish, **158, 487**
Golden headed goby, **632**
Golden-headed sleeper, **474, 476**
Golden jack, **424, 425**
Golden-spot spinefoot, **94**
Golden-striped grouper, **256, 652**
Gomphosus varius, **142, 143**, 577, **585, 586, 587, 852**
Goniistius, 251
Goniistius fuscus, **245, 246**
Goniistius gibbosus, **246, 251, 964**
Goniistius quadricornis, **247**, 481, **964**
Goniistius zebra, **247**
Goniistius zonatus, **248, 249**, 481, **964, 965**
Goosefishes, 508
Gorgasia maculata, **1401**
Grammistes sexlineatus, **256, 257, 652, 1227**
Grammistes sp., **256**
Grammistops ocellatus, **1482**
Gray puffer, **406**
Greasy grouper, **493**
Green clingfish, **165**
Green puffer, **405**
Greenling, **540, 541**
Groupers, 251, 489, 643
Grunions, 1412
Grunts, 222, 1507
Guam scorpionfish, **518**
Guitarfishes, 1073
Gymnapogon urospilotus, **1443**
Gymnocaesio, **1503**
Gymnocranius griseus, **1302, 1315**
Gymnocranius microdon, **1302**
Gymnothorax favagineus, **354**
Gymnothorax fimbriatus, **1002**
Gymnothorax flavimarginatus, **1000, 1407**
Gymnothorax kidako, **274, 354**
Gymnothorax leucostigma, **274, 351**
Gymnothorax meleagris, **1000, 1408**
Gymnothorax pictus, **1001, 1402**
Gymnothorax thyrsoidea, **1406**

Gymnothorax undulatus, **354**, **1001**, **1407**
Gymnothorax xanthostomus, **353**
Gymnothorax zonipectus, **350**, **1404**
Gymnothorax sp., **1403**, **1405**, **1406**
Gymnura japonica, **505**

H

Hairtail blenny, **466**
Halaelurus analis, **1081**
Half-and-half goatfish, **272**
Half-and-half wrasse, **145**, **583**
Halfbeak, **331**
Halfbeaks, 925
Half-striped angelfish, **19**
Halichoeres, 601
Halichoeres argus, **455**, **902**
Halichoeres bimaculatus, **600**
Halichoeres biocellatus, **454**, **901**
Halichoeres centiquadrus, **147**, **454**, **455**, **604**, **605**, **606**, **607**, **907**, **908**, **909**, **1574**
Halichoeres hoeveni, **603**
Halichoeres kawarin, **610**, **611**, **906**
Halichoeres leparensis, **904**
Halichoeres margaritaceus, **455**, **906**, **907**, **1575**
Halichoeres marginatus, **143**, **900**, **901**
Halichoeres melanochir, **602**, **910**
Halichoeres miniatus, **903**
Halichoeres nebulosus, **910**
Halichoeres nigrescens, **601**
Halichoeres notopsis, **603** (= *Halichoeres marginatus*)
Halichoeres poecilopterus, **137**, **451**, **899**
Halichoeres scapularis, **454**, **608**, **609**, **905**
Halichoeres trimaculatus, **904**
Halieutaea fumosa, **526**
Halieutaea retifera, 525
Halieutaea stellata, **526** (See *Halieutaea fumosa*)
Halieutaea stellata, **1092**, **1093**
Haliophis guttatus, **638**
Halmablennius lineatus, **1338**
Hammerhead sharks, 1087
Hapalogenys mucronatus, **1310**
Hapalogenys nigripinnis, **237**, **1310**
Hardwicke's wrasse, **146**
Hardyheads, 1412
Harengula, **1413**
Harengula koningsbergeri, **1048**
Harlequin sweetlips, **345**, **346**
Harlequin wrasse, **450**, **451**
Harpadon microchir, **912**
Harpadon translucens, **912**
HARPADONTIDAE, 913
Hawaiian lionfish, **513**
Hawaiian squirrelfish, **340**
Hawaiian triggerfish, 114
Hawaiian turkeyfish, **524**
Hawkfishes, 155, 660, 1143
Helicolenus hilgendorfi, **268**
Helicolenus sp., **952**
Hemigymnus, 577
Hemigymnus fasciatus, **144**, **582**
Hemigymnus melapterus, **145**, **583**, **584**, **864**
Hemipteronotus pentadactylus, **446**, **865**
Hemipteronotus taeniourus, **445**, **1568**
Hemipteronotus verrens, **865**
Hemipteronotus sp., **865**
Hemirhamphus commersoni, **1415**
Hemiramphus sajori, **331**
Hemiscyllium indicum, 1083
Hemitaurichthys polylepis, **41**, **1214**
Hemitaurichthys zoster, **768**, **769**
Heniochus, 39, 75, 761
Heniochus acuminatus, **38**, **39**, **69**, **75**, **368**, **369**, 761, **1209**, **1210**
Heniochus chrysostomus, **70**, **1212**, **1213**, **1529**
Heniochus monoceros, **71**, **72**, **1210**
Heniochus permutatus, **70**
Heniochus pleurotaenia, 761, **766**, **767**
Heniochus singularis, **70**, **1210**, **1211**
Heniochus varius, **70**, **369**, **767**, **1206**, **1207**, **1208**
Herald's angelfish, **8**, **18**, **19**
Herrings, 313
HETERODONTIDAE, 504
Heterodontus japonicus, **507**
Heterodontus zebra, **506**, **1085**, **1086**
Hexagrammos otakii, **540**
Hilu, **448**
Hippocampus coronatus, **211**, **212**
Hippocampus japonicus, **211**
Hippocampus kuda, **209**, **211**, **326**
Hippocampus mohnikei, **210**
Hippocampus sp., **214**
Hirundichthys oxycephalus, **923**
Histiopterus, 1217
Histiopterus acutirostris, **1216**, 1217
Histiopterus typus, **1216**
Histrio histrio, 259, **271**, **1366**
Holacanthus, 7
Holacanthus arcuatus, **364**
Holacanthus trimaculatus, **27**, **364**
Holacanthus venustus, **17**
HOLOCENTRIDAE, 230, 689
Holocentrus, 230, 689
Hologymnosus semidiscus, **145**, **447**, **592**, **874**, **875**
Holorhinus tobijei, **1076**
Holotrachys, 689
Honey jack, **430**
Honeycomb grouper, **493**, **1244**
Hoplolatilus sp., **1590**
Hornfishes, 391
Hughichthys, 663
Humphead wrasse, **574**
Humuhumunukunuku-a-puaa, 114, **116**
Hyperoglyphe, 1220
Hyperoglyphe japonica, 1220
Hypoatherina tsurugae, **316**
Hypseleotris guentheri, **1602**

I

Ichthyoscopus lebeck, **983**
Icichthys, 1220
Icichthys lockingtoni, 1220
Indian little fish, **240**, **462**
Indian wrasse, **445**
Indicus frogfish, **529**
Indigo wrasse, **443**
Iniistius dea, **450**, **866**
Iniistius pavo, **132**
Inimicus didactylum, **268**, **270** (See *Rhinopias argoliba*)
Inimicus japonicus, **515**, **536**
Isobuna, 660
Istiblennius, 636
Istiblennius coronatus, **471**
Istiblennius edentulus, **1339**
Istiblennius lineatus, **1338**
Istiblennius meleagris, **1339**
Istiblennius sp., **1337**
ISTIOPHORIDAE, 1257
Istiophorus platypterus, **1259**

J

Jacks, 423
Jacopever, **520**
Japanese bigeye, **551**, **552**
Japanese blanquillo, **532**
Japanese butterfly ray, **505**
Japanese butterflyfish, **66**
Japanese catshark, **503**
Japanese common eel, **351**
Japanese conger eel, **275**, **352**
Japanese diamond skate, **505**
Japanese horse mackerel, **432**
Japanese parrotfish, **543**, **544**, **545**
Japanese puffer, **108**
Japanese sea horse, **211**
Japanese soldierfish, **229**
Japanese star-gazer, **541**
Japanese stingfish, **523**
Japanese stingray, **509**
Japanese swallow, **17**
Japanese wrasse, **130**
John Dory, **550**
Johnius, 1319
Julis musume, **133**

K

Kentrocapros aculeatus, **414**
Keyhole angelfish, **25**, **363**
Kidako moray eel, **354**
Klein's butterflyfish, **41**, **374**
Knifejaws, 543
Kohler's grouper, **261**
Koran angelfish, **14**, **15**, **366**
Kryptophanaron alfredi, 1411
Kuhlia, 308
Kuhlia sandvicensis, 308
Kuhlia taeniura, **236**, **308**, **791**
KUHLIIDAE, 308
Kupipi, **194**
Kuweh, **430**
KYPHOSIDAE, 433, 1163
Kyphosus, 433, 1163

Kyphosus cinerascens, **237**, **1162**, **1163**
Kyphosus lembus, **1162**

L

Labracinus, 156
Labracinus cyclophthalmus, **156**, **157**, **1262**, **1263**
Labracoglossa argentiventris, **419**
Labrichthys, 587
Labrichthys unilineata, **594**, **595**, **862**
LABRIDAE, 128, 569
Labroides, 39, 128, 587
Labroides bicolor, **136**, **593**, **861**
Labroides dimidiatus, **129**, **136**, 159, **255**, **453**, **651**, **588**, **861**, **1487**, **1545**, **1580**, **1581**
Labroides phthirophagus, **340**
Labroides sp. cf *phthirophagus*, **453**
Labropsis sp., **1581**
Lace-finned filefish, **117**, **399**
Lactoria cornuta, **102**, **413**, **1364**
Lactoria diaphanus, **415**
Lactoria fornasina, **103**
Lagocephalus lunaris, **405**
Lamarck's angelfish, **19**
Lampris regia, **323**
Lancetfishes, 1257
Lantern-eyes, 1411
Large-scale saury, **338**
Lateolabrax japonicus, **336**, **1252**
Lates calcarifer, **1235**
Left-eyed flounders, **262**
LEIOGNATHIDAE, 1165
Leiognathus, 1165
Leiognathus equulus, **1164**
Leiognathus nuchilis, **236**
Leiognathus rivulatus, **1164**, **1166**
Lemonpeel, 8, **20**, **363**
Leopard moray, **354**
Leopard shark, **507**
Leopard wrasse, **456**
Lepadichthys frenatus, **165**
Lepidotrigla microptera, **536**, **1007**
Lepidotrigla sp., **1008**
Lepidozygus, 717
Lepidozygus anthioides, **716**, **717**
Leptocephalus, 260
Leptoscarus vaigiensis, **628**, **993**
Leptosynanceia, 959
LETHRINIDAE, 663, 666
Lethrinus choerorhynchus, **435**
Lethrinus chrysostomus, **1514**
Lethrinus fletus, **1298**, **1299**
Lethrinus harak, **1301**
Lethrinus kallopterus, **1300**
Lethrinus leutjanus, **1300**
Lethrinus miniatus, **1297**
Lethrinus reticulatus, **418**
Lethrinus variegatus, **1301**
Lethrinus xanthocheilus, **1301**
Lethrinus sp., **664**, **1514**
Lienardella fasciata, **450**, **451**, **879**, **1582**
Limanda schrenki, **1097**
Lined butterflyfish, **42**, **379**, **764**
Lionfish, 258, 653
Liopropoma lineata, **1481**
Liopropoma susumi, **1481**
Liopropoma sp., **1480**, **1481**
LIPARIDAE, 168
Lizardfish, 719
Lizardfishes, 335
Lo vulpinus, **92**, **93**, **95**
Loach gobies, 172
Lobotes pacificus, 1265
Lobotes surinamensis, **1265**
LOBOTIDAE, 1265
Long-barbeled goatfish, **343**
Long-finned batfish, 78, **79**, **81**
Long-finned caprodon, **496**
Longhorned cowfish, **102**, **413**
Long-jawed squirrelfish, **234**
Long-jawed wrasse, **441**
Long-nosed butterflyfish, **68**, **370**, **770**
Lopez' unicornfish, **389**
LOPHIIDAE, 508
Lophiomus setigerus, **508**, **509**
Lophonectes, 262
Lotella maximowiczi, **170**
LUTJANIDAE, 221, 673
Lutjanus, 221, 629
Lutjanus argentimaculatus, **1280**
Lutjanus bohar, **672**, **1516**
Lutjanus carponotatus, **1279**
Lutjanus chrysotaenia, **226**
Lutjanus erythropterus, **1284**, **1285**
Lutjanus flavipes, **1278**
Lutjanus fulviflamma, **226**, **1287**, **1288**, **1289**
Lutjanus gibbus, **672**, **1277**, **1518**
Lutjanus janthinuropterus, **1283**, **1285**
Lutjanus johni, **673**, **1282**
Lutjanus kasmira, 221, **226**, **227**, **1279**, **1516**
Lutjanus lineolatus, **1288**
Lutjanus lutjanus, **1515**
Lutjanus nematophorus, 221
Lutjanus quinquelineatus, **1278**, **1517**
Lutjanus rivulatus, **1280**
Lutjanus russelli, **1276**
Lutjanus sanguineus, **672**
Lutjanus sebae, 221, **674**, **1518**
Lutjanus semicinctus, **1281**
Lutjanus spilurus, **1278**
Lutjanus superbus, **1286**
Lutjanus vaigiensis, **1282**
Lutjanus vitta, **436**, **1289**
Lutjanus sp., **226**, **672**, **1290**
Lyretail coralfish, **489**, **490**
Lyretail wrasse, **457**

M

Mackerels, 1325
Macolor niger, **349**, **674**, **1276**
Macolor niger, 228
(See *Gaterin picus*)
Macolor sp., **1519**
Macropharyngodon meleagris, **877**, **878**
Macropharyngodon pardalis, **456**, **876**, **877**
Macropharyngodon varialvus, **624**
Macropharyngodon sp., **456**, **878**
MACRORHAMPHOSIDAE, 319
Macrorhamphosus scolopax, **322**
Magpie morwong, **246**, 251
Makaira indica, **1259**
Makaira mazara, **1259**
Malacanthus latovittatus, **135**, **531**
Malakichthys wakiyai, **1230**
Malamaima, **448**
Mandarin fish, **219**, **482**, **484**, **485**
Man-O-War fishes, 416
Manta birostris, **1397**
Marine plotosid catfishes, 333
Marlins, 1257
Masked butterflyfish, **71**, **72**
Max's cod, **170**
Megalaspis cordyla, **1058**
MEGALOPIDAE, 1041
Megalops cyprinoides, **1041**
Meiacanthus, 159, 1591
Meiacanthus atrodorsalis, **163**, **470**, **1592**
Meiacanthus atrodorsalis oualanensis, **470**, **1593**
Meiacanthus grammistes, **469**, **1335**, **1594**
Meiacanthus grammistes, **164**
(See *Meiacanthus kamoharai*)
Meiacanthus kamoharai, **164**
Meiacanthus kamoharai, **469**
(See *Meiacanthus grammistes*)
Meiacanthus mossambicus, **469**, **637**
Meiacanthus sp., **1593**
Melichthys, 815
Melichthys indicus, **397**
Melichthys ringens, **397**
(See *Melichthys indicus*)
Melichthys vidua, **118**, **120**, **1628**
Mempachi, 230
Mene maculata, **1167**, 1168
MENIDAE, 1167
Merinthe macrocephalus, **953**
Merten's butterflyfish, **63**
Meuschenia skottowei, **121**
Meyer's butterflyfish, **756**, **758**
Microcanthus strigatus, 74, **76**, **480**, **1178**
MICRODESMIDAE, 172, 633
Midnight angelfish, **362**
Milkfish, 1044
Milletseed butterflyfish, **374**
Mimic blenny, 159
Minous monodactylus, **958**
Minous versicolor, **958**
Mirolabrichthys, 643
Mirolabrichthys dispar, **1472**, **1473**, **1476**
Mirolabrichthys evansi, **648**, **650**, **651**
Mirolabrichthys tuka, **422**, **1383**, **1474**, **1475**

Mobula diabolus, **1075**
MOBULIDAE, 1075
Mojarras, 917
MONACANTHIDAE, 122, 819, 1351
Monacanthus chinensis, **400**
Monacanthus filicauda, **1355**
Monacanthus mosaicus, **399**
Monkfishes, 1069
MONOCENTRIDAE, 260
Monocentris gloriaemaris, 260
Monocentris japonica, 260, **273**, **1158**, **1159**
MONODACTYLIDAE, 74
Monodactylus argenteus, 74, **76**, **312**
Monodactylus sebae, 74
Monotaxis, **642**, 664
Monotaxis grandoculis, **435**, **662**, **663**, **664**, **665**, **1500**
Moonfishes, 74, **312**, 1167
Moorish idol, 75, **77**, 810
Moray eels, 260, 1403
MORINGUIDAE, 1410
Moringua microchir, **1409**, **1410**
Morwongs, 251
Mosaic leatherjacket, 399
Mottled blenny, **472**
Mudskippers, 172
Mugil cephalus, 313, **314**, **315**, **316**
MUGILIDAE, 313
MUGILOIDIDAE, 777
Mullets, 313
MULLIDAE, 259, 739, 1461
Mulloidichthys, 259, 739
Mulloidichthys auriflamma, 342, **980**, **1460**
Mulloidichthys pflugeri, **980**
Mulloidichthys samoenis, **739**, **1461**, **1465**
Mullus, 259
Mullus surmuletus, 1461
Muraenesox cinereus, **351**
MURAENIDAE, 260, 1403
Mustard surgeonfish, **384**
Mylio latus, **437**
Mylio macrocephalus, **237**, **438**
MYLIOBATIDAE, 1074
Myliobatus tobijei, **1076**
Myripristis, 230, 689
Myripristis argyromus, **1064**
Myripristis bowditchae, **1064**
Myripristis kuntee, **233**, **340**
Myripristis murdjan, 230, **232**, **1064**, **1450**
Myripristis pralinus, **341**, **695**, **1450**
Myripristis violaceus, **341**, **694**, **1449**, **1450**
Myripristis vittatus, **1449**
Myripristis sp., **231**, **1617**

N

Narke japonica, **1067**
Naso, 84, 793
Naso brevirostris, **389**, 807, 808, **1153**, **1154**, **1612**
Naso lituratus, **89**, **90**, **390**, **804**, **805**, **806**, **1155**
Naso lopezi, **389**
Naso unicornis, **89**, **388**, **807**, **1152**, **1153**, **1154**
Naso sp., **808**
Naucrates, 423
Naucrates ductor, **1059**
Navodon ayraud, **1356**
Navodon modestus, **126**, **1352**
Needlefishes, 329
Nematalosa japonica, **1047**
Nemateleotris magnificus, 173, **176**, **1011**
Nemateleotris sp., **1603**
NEMIPTERIDAE, 666, 1493
Nemipterus, 666, 1493
Nemipterus bathybus, **439**, **1294**
Nemipterus ovenii, **1303**
Nemipterus virgatus, **439**, **1293**
Neoclinus bryope, **163**
Neoditrema ransonneti, 355, **337**
Neopercis aurantiaca, **467**
Neopercis multifasciatus, **468**
Neopercis sexfasciata, **468**
Network filefish, **127**, **398**, **408**
Nibblers, 433
Nibea albiflora, **1320**
Nibea goma, **1321**
Nibea mitsukurii, **1320**
Niphobles puffer, **113**, **408**
Niphon spinosus, **544**
NOMEIDAE, 416, 1220
Nomeus gronovii, **417**
Novaculichthys taeniourus, **149**

O

Oblong filefish, **126**
Oblong scorpionfish, **520**
Oceanic sea horse, **211**, **326**
Ocellate butterflyfish, **62**, **65**
Ocycrius japonicus, **418**
Odonus niger, **119**, **395**, **1344**
OGCOCEPHALIDAE, 525
Omobranchus elegans, **162**, **473**
One-band snapper, **436**
One-line rainbow wrasse, **135**
Onigocia spinosa, **539**
Opah, **323**
OPHIDIIDAE, 997
Ophioblennius, 160
Ophiocara sp., **1598**
Opistognathus sp., 1401
OPLEGNATHIDAE, 543
Oplegnathus fasciatus, **543**, **544**, **545**
Oplegnathus punctatus, **547**
Oplopomus sp., **1600**
Orange-finned anemonefish, **191**
Orange gurnard, **535**
Orange-ring batfish, 78, **80**, **355**
Orbiculate cardinalfish, **243**
ORECTOLOBIDAE, 501, 1399
Orectolobus, 1399
Orectolobus japonicus, **503**, **1082**
Orectolobus ogilby, **501**, **502**
Oriental sweetlips, **347**
Oriole angelfish, **26**
Ornate butterflyfish, **59**, **64**
Ornate goby, **475**
Ostichthys, 230, 689
Ostichthys japonicus, **229**, 230
Ostorhinchus angustatus, **687**
Ostorhinchus endekataenia, **686**, **687**
Ostorhinchus fleurieu, **966**
Ostorhinchus sp., **687**
Ostracion cubicus, **99**, **100**, **101**, **1362**, **1638**
Ostracion meleagris, **101**, **1364**
Ostracion tuberculatus, **1637**
OSTRACIONTIDAE, 97
Oval-spot butterflyfish, **41**, **373**
Oxycirrhites, 660, 663, 1143
Oxycirrhites typus, 155, 660, **1619**
Oxymonacanthus, 821
Oxymonacanthus longirostris, **115**, **820**, **821**, **1633**
Oxyurichthys papuensis, **479**

P

Pacific hogfish, **143**
Paddlefin wrasse, **134**
Painted blenny, **166**
Painted coral bass, **490**
Painted sweetlips, **224**
Palani, **385**
Palau squirrelfish, **341**
Pampus, 1220
Pampus argenteus, **1219**, 1220
Pampus chinensis, 1220
Paopao, **424**
Papuan goby, **479**
Papyrichthys pellucidus, **419** (See *Psenes pellucidus*)
Paracallionymus, 219
Paracanthurus, 797
Paracanthurus hepatus, 85, **87**, **381** frontispiece (Book II), **1148**, **1613**
Paracentropogon longispinis, **517**
Paracentropogon rubripinnis, **518**, **536**
Parachaetodon ocellatus, **65**
Paracheilinus filamentosus, **1570**, **1571**
Paracirrhites, 155, 660
Paracirrhites arcatus, **155**, **660**, **661**
Paracirrhites forsteri, **157**, **1142**, **1618**, **1620**
Paracirrhites typee, **488**
Paralichthys olivaceus, **1095**
Paraluteres, 821
Paraluteres prionurus, **401**, **824**, **1353**, **1635**
Paraluteres sp., **401**
Paramia quinquelineata, **240**, **683**
Paramonacanthus barnardi, **822**
Paramonacanthus oblongus, **126**
PARAPERCIDAE, 467, 777
Parapercis, 777
Parapercis cephalopunctatus, **777**, **778**, **779**, **932**
Parapercis clathrata, **932**, **1422**

Parapercis cylindrica, **776**, **777**, **932**, **1422**
Parapercis multifasciatus, **166**
Parapercis nebulosus, **933**
Parapercis pulchellus, **468**, **473**, **933**
Parapercis sexfasciatus, **167**
Parapercis tetracantha, **934**, **1421**
Paraplagusia japonica, **1100**
Parapriacanthus, 251
Parapriacanthus dispar, **1418**, **1419**
Parapristopoma, **1290**
Parapterurus heterurus, **948**
Parascorpaena, 653, **1626**
Parascorpaena aurita, **654**
Parascorpaena picta, **955**
Paristiopterus, 1217
Parmaturus sp., **1091**
Parrotfishes, 151, 626
Parupeneus, 739
Parupeneus barberinoides, **272**, **343**, **344**
Parupeneus barberinus, **979**, **1466**
Parupeneus bifasciatus, **1462**, **1463**, **1464**
Parupeneus chryseredros, **975**, **740**, **1465**, **1466**
Parupeneus chrysopleuron, **972**
Parupeneus cyclostomas, **974-5**, **740**
Parupeneus fraterculus, **972**, **973**
Parupeneus indicus, **978**
Parupeneus macronemus, **343**, **741**
Parupeneus pleurospilus, **978**
Parupeneus pleurotaenia, **973**
Parupeneus trifasciatus, 272, **342**, **976**, **977**
Parupeneus sp., **1466**
Pastel razorfish, **450**
Pataecus fronto, **962**
Peacock grouper, **499**
Peacock wrasse, **137**, **451**
Pearlfishes, 510
Pearlscale razorfish, **149**
Pearl-scaled angelfish, **20**, **365**
Pearly monocle-bream, **422**
Pegasus volitans, **218**
Pelates quadrilineatus, **1317**
Pelecanichthys, 262
Pen shell pearlfish, **510**
PEMPHERIDAE, 245
Pempheris, 245, 251
Pempheris japonicus, **1221**
Pempheris klunzingeri, **1223**
Pempheris oualensis, 245, **487**, **1223**
Pempheris schwenki, **698**
Pempheris vanicolensis, **1418**
Pempheris xanthoptera, **244**
Pempheris sp., **487**
Pennant butterflyfish, **69**, **368**, **369**
Pentaceropsis, 1217
Pentaceros, 1217
Pentaceros japonicus, **1217**, **1218**
PENTACEROTIDAE, 1217
PENTAPODIDAE, 666
Pentapodus caninus, **1308**, **1501**
Pentapodus nemurus, **1501**
Peprilus, 1220
Percanthias japonicus, **1224**
Periophthalmus, 172
Periophthalmus cantonensis, **177**
Periophthalmus papilio, **177**
Peristedion nierstraszi, **1006**
Pervagor, 821
Pervagor melanocephalus, **117**, **399**, **1353**, **1631**
Pervagor spilosoma, **397**
Pervagor tomentosus, **400**
Petrocheiliops sp., **1601**
Petroscirtes, 636
Petroscirtes breviceps, **164**, **1330**
Petroscirtes mitratus, **639**
Philippine butterflyfish, **57**
Pholidichthys leucotaenia, **164**, **420**, **1428**
Photoblepharon palpebratus, 1411
Pinecone fishes, 260, **273**
Pink-barred weever, **467**
Pink-tailed triggerfish, **118**, **120**
Pipefishes, 208, 1420
Plagiotremus rhinorhynchos, **160**, **161**, **1591**, **1594**
Plagiotremus tapeinosoma, **471**
Plagiotremus sp., **636**
PLATACIDAE, 78, 1138
Platacinae, 1138, 1141
Platax batavianus, 78
Platax orbicularis, 78, **82**, **83**, **356**, **357**, **358**, **1136**, **1137**
Platax pinnatus, 78, **80**, **355**, **1531**, **1533**
Platax teira, 78, **79**, **81**, **1138**, **1532**
Platichthys stellatus, 263
PLATYCEPHALIDAE, 538
Platycephalus crocodilus, **541**, **1006**
Platycephalus indicus, **1004**
Platycephalus grandidieri, 775
Platycephalus sp., **775**
Platyrhina sinensis, **1077**
Plectropomus, 643
Plectropomus leopardus, **1232**, **1488**
Plectropomus maculatus, **1232**, **1233**
Plectropomus oligacanthus, **1483**
Plectrypops, 230
PLESIOPIDAE, 156
Plesiops coeruleolineatus, **1480**
Pleurogrammus azonus, **541**
PLEURONECTIDAE, 262
Pleuronichthys cornutus, **1097**
PLOTOSIDAE, 333
Plotosus, 333
Plotosus anguillaris, 271, **333**, **334**, **1428**, **1429**
Poecilopora, 641
Pogonoculius zebra, **179**, **472**, **1012**
Polkadot grouper, **256**, **527**
Polymixia, 1173
Polymixia japonica, 1173, **1174**
Polymixia lowei, 1173
Polymixia nobilis, 1173
POLYMIXIIDAE, 1173
POMACANTHIDAE, 7, 781
Pomacanthus, 7, 781
Pomacanthus annularis, **26**, **367**
Pomacanthus imperator, **8**, **9**, **10**, **11**, **12**, **13**, **786**, **787**, **788**, **1114**, **1115**, **1116**, **1117**, **1538**, **1539**
Pomacanthus semicirculatus, 12, **14**, **15**, **366**, **1117**, **1118**, **1536**, **1537**, **1539**
POMACENTRIDAE, 181, 289, 701, 1545
Pomacentrus alexanderae, **1563**
Pomacentrus amboinensis, **201**, **305**, **1030**
Pomacentrus bankanensis, **1028**, **1029**, **1559**
Pomacentrus coelestis, **197**, **203**, **1555**, **1562**
Pomacentrus dorsalis, **201**, **1027**
Pomacentrus lepidogenys, **1563**
Pomacentrus melanochir, **726**
Pomacentrus moluccensis, **201**
(See *Pomacentrus amboinensis*)
Pomacentrus nigricans, **719**, **720**, **774**
Pomacentrus nigromarginatus, **1560**
Pomacentrus notophthalmus, **1557**
Pomacentrus pavo, **725**, **1027**
Pomacentrus perspicillatus, **1560**
Pomacentrus popei, **1032**, **1554**
Pomacentrus pulcherrimus, **726**
Pomacentrus reidi, **1562**
Pomacentrus sufflavus, **1026**
Pomacentrus taeniurus, **724**, **725**
Pomacentrus trichourus, **721**
Pomacentrus tripunctatus, **722**, **723**
Pomacentrus vaiuli, **304**
Pomacentrus sp., **206**
(See *Abudefduf cyaneus*)
Pomacentrus sp., **1033**
POMADASYIDAE, 222, 666, 1507
Pomadasys hasta, **1311**
Pomadasys maculatus, **1311**
POMATOMIDAE, 1266
Pomatomus saltatrix, **1266**
Pomfrets, 416, 1170, 1220
Pompanos, 423
Ponyfish, 1165
Popeyed sea goblin, **268**
Porcupinefish, **410**, **411**
Porcupinefishes, 96
Porgies, 433
Porky, **127**
Port and starboard light fish, 260
Port Jackson sharks, 504
Portuguese man-o-war fish, **417**
Powder-blue surgeonfish, 85, **381**
Praealticus, 1337
Pranesus pinguis, **1412**
Premnas biaculeatus, **190**, **301**, **1389**, 1545, **1546**, **1547**
PRIACANTHIDAE, 231, 551
Priacanthus cruentatus, **231**, **1065**, **1068**
Priacanthus hamrur, **552**, **696**, **697**
Priacanthus macracanthus, **248**
Priacanthus sp., **1458**
Prickly leatherjacket, **398**
Prionurus, 84, 797

Prionurus microlepidotus, 88
Pristiapogon snyderi, 685
Pristigenys niphonius, **551**, **552**, **1065**
Pristiophorus japonicus, **1079**
Pristipomoides argyrogrammicus, **1291**
Pristipomoides filamentosus, **1292**
Pristis cuspidatus, **1079**
Prometheichthys prometheus, **929**
Protoxotes, 328
Psenes indicus, **1221**
Psenes pellucidus, **419**, **1221**
Psenopsis, 1220
Psenopsis anomala, **417**, 1220
Psettodes erumei, **1096**
Pseudamia, 1432
Pseudamia gelatinosa, **1439**
Pseudanthias taira, **239**
Pseudobalistes, 815
Pseudobalistes fuscus, **117**, **125**, **394**, **1343**
Pseudoblennius cottoides, **166**
Pseudoblennius percoides, **166**
Pseudocheilinus evanidus, **456**, **1579**
Pseudocheilinus hexataenia, **449**, **625**, **853**, **1579**
Pseudocheilinus octotaenia, **449**
Pseudocheilinus tetrataenia, **449**
Pseudocheilinus sp., **625**
PSEUDOCHROMIDAE, 156
Pseudochromis, 156
Pseudochromis aureus, **1264**
Pseudochromis cyanotaenia, **1264**
Pseudochromis fuscus, **1477**
Pseudochromis melanotaenia, **1262**, **1264**
Pseudochromis paccagnellae, **1478**, **1479**
Pseudochromis xanthochir, **1478**
Pseudodax moluccanus, **443**, **1569**
Pseudogramma polyacantha, **1482**
Pseudolabrus gracilis, **130**
Pseudolabrus japonicus, **130**, **878**, **896**, **897**
Pseudoplesiops sargeanti, **1480**
Pseudopristipoma nigra, **1272**
Pseudorhombus cinnamoneus, **276**
Pseudupeneus, 259, 739
Pseudupeneus chryseredros, **470**, **740**
Pseudupeneus cyclostomas, **740**
Pseudupeneus macronema, **741**
(These **Pseudupeneus** species are now considered under **Parupeneus**)
Psychedelic fish, **220**, **483**, **484**
PTERACLIDAE, 1173
Pteragogus flagellifera, **132**, **148**, **892**, **893**
Pteragogus sp., **132**
Ptereleotris microlepis, **477**
Ptereleotris tricolor, **476**, **477**, **1012**, **1013**
Ptereleotris splendidum, **173**, **176**
(See *Nemateleotris magnificus*)
Pterocaesio diagramma, **1296**
Pterocaesio tile, **676**, **1295**, **1502**, **1504**
Pterogobius zonoleucus, **179**
Pterois, 258, 653
Pterois antennata, **263**, **265**, **657**, **658**, **944**
Pterois lunulata, **264**, **512**, **514**, **938**, **939**
Pterois radiata, **513**, **944**, **1622**
Pterois sphex, **513**
Pterois volitans, **265**, **512**, **940**, **941**, **942**, **943**, **1622**, **1623**
Pterothrissus gissu, **1043**
Puffers, 94, 114
Purple flying gurnard, **534**
Purple queen, **422**
Purple surgeonfish, **384**
Pygoplites, 786
Pygoplites diacanthus, **24**, **25**, **789**, **790**, **1125**, **1534**, **1537**

Q

Quinquarius japonicus, 1217

R

Rabbitfishes, 93
Raccoon butterflyfish, **50**, **51**
RACHYCENTRIDAE, 1323
Rachycentron canadum, **1322**, **1323**
Raffles' butterflyfish, **52**
Rainbow wrasse, **612**
Razorfish, 319, **320**, **321**, **866**
Razor-trevally, 1167
Rectangle triggerfish, **117**, **394**
Red clownfish, **184**, **187**
Red grouper, **491**, **492**
Red gurnard, **537**
Red morwong, **245**, **246**
Red parrotfish, **459**
Red rattlefish, **526**
Red-shoulder wrasse, **131**, **452**
Red soldierfish, **341**
Red-spotted grouper, **491**
Red-spotted razorfish, **446**
Red-striped wrasse, **133**
Red-tailed wrasse, **440**
Red-tooth triggerfish, **119**, **395**
Red wasp-fish, **518**, **536**
Reef stonefish, **521**
Regal angelfish, **24**, **25**, **790**
Remora albescens, **935**
Remora sp., **236**
Requiem sharks, **1087**
Reticulated butterflyfish, **43**, **377**
Reticulated damselfish, **205**
Reticulated puffer, **105**, **407**
Reticulated wrasse, **456**
Rhabdosargus sarba, **1314**
Rhina ancylostomus, **1072**, **1073**
Rhinchichthys, 230
Rhinecanthus, 815
Rhinecanthus aculeatus, **116**, **817**, **1346**, **1628**, **1629**
Rhinecanthus assasi, **125**
(See *Rhinecanthus verrucosus*)
Rhinecanthus rectangulus, **117**, **394**, **1347**
Rhinecanthus verrucosus, **125**, **1348**
RHINOBATIDAE, 1073
Rhinobatos formosensis, **1071**
Rhinobatos hynnicephalus, **1071**
Rhinogobius brunneus, **1015**
Rhinomuraena amboinensis, **275**, **350**, **998**
Rhinomuraena quaesita, **275**, **999**, **1409**
Rhinopias argoliba, **268**, **270**
Rhinoplagusia japonica, **1100**
Rhynchocymba nystromi, **352**
Richardson's dragonet, **486**
Right-eyed flounders, 262
Rock blenny, **470**
Rouge fish, **517**
Round batfish, **82**, **83**, **356**, **357**, **358**
Ruby scat, **310**
Rudarius ercodes, **127**, **398**, **408**
Rudderfish, **429**, **432**
Rudderfishes, 433, 1163
Russet angelfish, **363**
Rusty angelfish, **1**, **20**, **21**
Ruvettus pretiosus, **929**

S

Sabre-tooth blenny, **161**, **471**
Sacura margaritacea, **238**, **1225**
Saddle butterflyfish, **44**, **46-47**, **49**, **375**
Saddle-back clownfish, **183**
Saddled filefish, **401**
Saddled puffer, **401**
Saddled rainbow wrasse, **455**
Sagamia genionema, **178**, **478**
Sailfin leaffish, **516**
Sailfin tang, **89**, **91**
Sailfishes, 1257
Salarias, 636
Salarias fasciatus, **639**, **1336**
Salarius lineatus, **1338**
Salmonet, **272**
Samaris cristatus, **1098**
Sandsmelt, **236**
Sarda orientalis, **1326**
Sardinella, **1413**
Sardinella aurita, **1046**
Sardinella sp., **1046**
Sardines, 313
Sardinops melanosticta, **315**, **317**
Sargassum fish, 259, **271**
Saurida, 335
Saurida gracilis, **916**, **1427**
Saurida undosquamis, **338**
Saury, **331**
Sawtooth boxfish, **441**
Sayonara satsumae, **1226**
Scaled blennies, 159
Scaleless blennies, 159
SCARIDAE, 151, 626
Scarlet anglerfish, **528**
Scarlet wrasse, **456**
Scarops rubroviolaceus, **986**, **987**, **1584**, **1587**

Scarus aeruginosus, **989**
Scarus bowersi, **988**
Scarus capristratoides, **988**
Scarus chlorodon, **630**
Scarus dubius, **989**
Scarus erythrodon, **1587**
Scarus fasciatus, **1588**
Scarus frenatus, **665**, **993**
Scarus ghobban, **153**, **154**, **990**, **991**, **992**
Scarus harid, **995**
Scarus janthochir, **988**
Scarus lepidus, **927**, **994**, **627**
Scarus madagascariensis, **629**
Scarus microrhinos, **154**, **987**
Scarus mus, **1589**
Scarus sexvittatus, **152**, **626**, **627**
Scarus troscheli, **1584**, **1585**
Scarus venosus, **458**
Scarus sp., **153**, **459**, **631**, **992**, **994**
SCATOPHAGIDAE, 309
Scatophagus, 309
Scatophagus argus, **309**, **310**, **311**, **1176**, **1177**
Scatophagus rubrifrons, 310, **1176**
Scats, 309, **312**
Schedophilus, 1220
Schedophilus maculatus, 1220
Schlegel's caprodon, **496**
SCIANIDAE, 1319
Scissortail, **476**, **477**
Scolopsis, 666, 1493, **1501**
Scolopsis bilineatus, 222, **223**, **421**, **668**, **1309**, 1493, **1495**, **1497**, **1499**
Scolopsis cancellatus, **1303**, **1309**, **1496**, **1498**
Scolopsis dubiosus, **421**
Scolopsis ghanam, **668**
Scolopsis margaritifer, **422**, **1496**, **1497**, **1498**
Scolopsis monogramma, **1304**, **1305**, **1306**
Scolopsis vosmeri, **1307**, **1308**
Scolopsis xenochrous, **1497**, **1499**
Scomber, 1325
Scomber japonicus, **1327**
Scomberomorus commerson, **1328**
Scomberomorus koreanus, **1328**
Scomberomorus niphonius, **1328**
Scomberomorus sinensis, **1328**
SCOMBRIDAE, 1325
Scombrops boops, **548**
Scorpaena izensis, **950**, **951**
Scorpaena neglecta, **268**, **270**, **949**
SCORPAENIDAE, 258, 511, 653, 959
Scorpaenodes, 653
Scorpaenodes guamensis, **518**, **957**
Scorpaenodes hirsutus, **1625**
Scorpaenodes littoralis, **957**
Scorpaenodes parvipinnis, **516**
Scorpaenopsis cirrhosa, **268**, **655**, **952**, **1626**
Scorpaenopsis gibbosa, **656**, **948**
Scorpaenopsis sp., **1626**
SCORPIDIDAE, 74
Scorpionfish, **266**, **269**
Scorpionfishes, 258, 511, 653, 959
Scorpionopsis, 653
Sea-bull, **70**, **369**
Sea horses, 208, 1420
Sea robins, 511
Sebastapistes, 653
Sebastapistes kowiensis, **656**
Sebastapistes oglinus, **655**
Sebastapistes sp., **1625**
Sebastes baramenuke, **954**
Sebastes inermis, **523**
Sebastes joyneri, **519**, **523**
Sebastes matsubarai, **954**
Sebastes nivosus, **519**, **522**
Sebastes oblongus, **520**, **955**
Sebastes pachycephalus, **956**
Sebastes schlegeli, **520**
Sebastes trivittatus, **522**
Sebastes vulpes, **520**
Sebasticus marmoratus, **266**, **267**
Sebasticus sp., **956**
Sebastolobus macrochir, **518**
Secutor, 1165
Secutor ruconius, **1165**
Selenotoca, 309
Semicossyphus reticulatus, **138**, **139**, **911**
Sergeant-major, **195**
Seriola aureovittata, **429**
Seriola dumerilii, **1059**
Seriola nigrofasciata, **1060**
Seriola purpurascens, **429**, **432**, **1059**
Seriola quinqueradiata, **427**, **428**
Seriolella, 1220
SERRANIDAE, 251, 489, 643
Serranocirrhitus, 660
Setipinna breviceps, **1049**
Sharp-nosed puffers, **96**, **98**, **823**
Short-nosed unicornfish, **389**
Short-snouted tripodfish, **392**
Short-spined scorpionfish, **516**
Shovel-nosed rays, **1073**
Shrimpfish, 319, **320**, **321**, **1416**, **1417**
Sicyopterus cf. *longifilis*, **1600**
Siderea picta, **1402**
SIGANIDAE, 93
Siganus corallinus, **390**
Siganus doliatus, **1616**
Siganus fuscascens, **388**
Siganus lineatus, **94**, **1615**
Siganus oramin, **95**, **1145**, **1614**
Siganus puellus, **1146**, **1614**
Siganus rostratus, **1146**
Siganus spinus, **1145**
Siganus stellatus, **809**
Siganus striolata, **1145**
Siganus vermiculatus, **389**
Siganus virgatus, **93**, **94**
Siganus sp., **1616**
Silky goby, **179**
SILLAGINIDAE, 1003
Sillago sihama, **236**, **1003**
Silver blanquillo, **533**
Silver conger eel, **352**
Silver squirrelfish, **339**
Silver sweeper, 245, **487**
Silversides, 1412
Singular butterflyfish, **70**
Siphamia, 241
Six-banded perch, **167**
Six-banded weever, **468**
Six-lined wrasse, **449**
Six-striped angelfish, **16**, **361**
Skipper, **174**
Skunk blenny, **170**
Skunk clownfish, **185**, **188**
Sleeper gobies, 172, 633
Slipmouths, 1165
Smooth dogfishes, 504
Smoothhead unicornfish, **89**, **90**, **390**
Snake eels, 262
Snake mackerels, 927
Snakefish, **336**
Snakeskin goby, **178**
Snappers, 221, 673
Snipefishes, 319
Snowflake moray eel, **353**
Snowfleck scorpionfish, **519**, **522**
Soapy, **236**
Solander's sharpnosed puffer, **402**
SOLEIDAE, 1099
Solenichthys sp., **215**
SOLENOSTOMIDAE, 214
Solenostomus, 214
Solenostomus paeginius, **216**, **217**
Soles, 1099
Spadefishes, 1138
Spaghetti eels, 1410
SPARIDAE, 433
Spearfishes, 1257
Speckled-fin flathead, **539**
Speckled-finned grouper, **497**
Speckled wrasse, **131**, **452**
Sphaeramia nematoptera, **243**, **464**, **465**, 1432, **1448**
Sphaeramia orbicularis, **969**, 1432, **1448**
Sphaeroides, 97
Sphyraena barracuda, **318**, **921**
Sphyraena japonica, **698**
Sphyraena pinguis, **318**
Sphyraena qenie, **921**
Sphyraena sp., **1414**
SPHYRAENIDAE, 925
Sphyrna blochii, **1090**
Sphyrna corona, **1090**
Sphyrna couardi, **1090**
Sphyrna lewini, **1090**
Sphyrna media, **1090**
Sphyrna mokarran, **1090**
Sphyrna tiburo, **1090**
Sphyrna tudes, **1090**
Sphyrna zygaena, **1089**, **1090**, **1091**
SPHYRNIDAE, 1087
Spikefishes, 391
Spilotichthys pictus, **224**, **348**, **1268**, **1270**, **1512**, **1513**
Spine-cheeked anemonefish, **190**
Spine-cheeked snapper, 222
Spiny-eyed cardinalfish, **460**

Spiny puffer, **103**
Spiny-tailed tang, **88**
Spot-banded butterflyfish, **53**
Spot bream, **667**
Spotfin lionfish, **263**
Spottail wrasse, **580**
Spot-tailed cardinalfish, **461**
Spotted boxfish, **99**
Spotted grouper, **254, 645**
Spotted halibut, **276**
Spotted hawkfish, **157**
Spotted knifejaw, **547**
Spotted rabbitfish, **95, 809**
Spotted scat, **309**
Spotted sharpnosed puffer, **402**
Spotted triggerfish, **120**
Spotted wrasse, **442**
Spottyback scorpionfish, **519, 523**
Springeratus xanthosoma, **1334**
Squatina japonica, **1070**
SQUATINIDAE, 1069
Squirrelfishes, 230, 689
Stanulus seychellensis, **472**
Stargazers, 538
Starry flounder, 263
Starry triggerfish, **395**
Stegostoma fasciatum, **1084, 1398, 1399**
Stephanolepis cirrhifer, **127, 1354**
Stereolepis ishinagi, 252, **541, 1234**
Stethojulis, **598**
Stethojulis albovittata, **599**
Stethojulis axillaris, **131, 146, 452, 598, 890**
Stethojulis interrupta, **890, 891**
Stethojulis kalosoma, **135**
Stethojulis phekadopleura, **889**
Stethojulis strigiventer, **596, 597**
Stethojulis trilineata, **889, 891**
Stichaeus grigorjewi, **466**
Stigmatogobius javanicus, **1599**
Stingaree, **509**
Stingrays, 509, 1393
Stonefish, **521**
Stretched silk goby, **175, 474**
Striped-belly puffer, **106, 107, 109**
Striped cardinalfish, **460**
Striped catfish, **271, 333, 334**
Striped goby, **174**
Striped grouper, **451**
Striped grunter, **229**
Striped jack, **431**
Striped morwong, **248, 249, 481**
Stripey, 74, **76, 480**
STROMATEIDAE, 416, 1220
Stromateus, 1220
Sufflamen, 815
Sufflamen bursa, **816, 1627**
Sufflamen chrysoptera, **120, 1628, 1629**
Sufflamen fraenatus, **120**
Sufflamen sp., **120**
Suggrundus meerdervoorti, **539, 1005**
Suggrundus sp., **1004, 1005**
Surfperch, **337**
Surfperches, 335
Surgeonfishes, 84, 793, 1607
Sweepers, 245
Sweeps, 74
Sweetlips, 222, 1507
Swordfish, 1260
Symphorichthys spilurus, **227**
Symphorus nematophorus, **227**
Synagrops, 678, 1432
Synanceia, 959
Synanceia horrida, **521**
Synanceia verrucosa, **521, 959, 960**
Synchiropus, 219, 220
Synchiropus lineolatus, **1331**
Synchiropus picturatus, 219, **220, 483, 484**
Synchiropus splendidus, **219, 220, 482, 484, 485**
Synchiropus sp., **218, 1331, 1332**
SYNGNATHIDAE, 208, 1420
Syngnathus schlegeli, **324**
SYNODONTIDAE, 335
Synodus, 335
Synodus indicus, **774**
Synodus variegatus, **338, 915, 1424, 1425, 1426, 1427**

T

Taenioconger hassi, **1400**
Taenionotus triacanthus, **516, 1624**
Taeniura lymma, **509, 1392, 1393**
Tahitian squirrelfish, **339**
Tail-light damselfish, **207**
Taius tumifrons, **438**
Taractes, 1173
Taractes longipinnis, **1172**
Tarpons, 1041
Tasselled wobbegong, **501, 502**
Tawny wrasse, **150**
Teardrop butterflyfish, **43**
TETRAGONURIDAE, 1220
Tetraodon, 97
TETRAODONTIDAE, 97
Tetrapterus audax, **1258**
Tetrosomus gibbosus, **412, 415**
Thalassoma, 618
Thalassoma amblycephalus, **134, 612, 614, 888, 889**
Thalassoma fuscum, **885**
Thalassoma hardwicke, **146, 616 617, 618, 619, 880, 881, 1575**
Thalassoma hebraicum, **457, 613**
Thalassoma janseni, **622, 886**
Thalassoma lunare, **457, 614, 615, 1572**
Thalassoma lutescens, **148, 149, 882, 883, 884, 1572, 1573**
Thalassoma quinquevittata, **620, 885, 886**
Thalassoma umbrostygma, **621, 886**
Therapon jarbua, 222, **1318**
Therapon oxyrhinchus, **228**
Therapon theraps, 222, **229, 1318**
THERAPONIDAE, 222
Thick-lipped blenny, **166**
Thick-lipped goby, **178**
Tholichthys, 39
Thornback cowfish, **103**
Thornbacked boxfish, **412, 415**
Threadfin, **426**
Threadfin cardinalfish, **460**
Thread-sail fishes, **913**
Three-bar goatfish, **342**
Three-lined wrasse, **891**
Three-spot angelfish, **27, 364**
Three-spot damselfish, **205**
Three-striped butterflyfish, **60-61**
Three-striped tigerfish, 222
Thrissa hamiltoni, **1048**
Thrush eels, 1410
Thunnus alalunga, **1324**
Thunnus obesus, **1324**
Thunnus thynnus, 1325, **1329**
Tiger puffer, **104**
Tigerfishes, 222
Tilefishes, 531
Tinker's butterflyfish, **378**
TORPEDINIDAE, 1067
Torpedo tokionis, **1068**
Torpedos, 1067
Toxotes, 328
Toxotes chatareus, **327, 328**
Toxotes jaculator, **327**
TOXOTIDAE, 327
Trachichthodes affinis, 1161
Trachinocephalus, 335, 959
Trachinocephalus myops, **336, 916**
Trachinotus bailloni, **430, 813**
Trachinotus blochii, **1459**
Trachurus japonicus, **432**
TRIACANTHIDAE, 391
Triacanthus aculeatus, 391
Triacanthus anomalus, **392**
Triacanthus biaculeatus, **391**
Triacanthus brevirostris, **392**
TRIAKIDAE, 504
Triakis scyllia, **507**
Triangle butterflyfish, **57, 378**
TRICHIURIDAE, 927
Trichiurus lepturus, **928**
Tridentiger trigonocephalus, **174**
Triggerfishes, 114, 815, **1630**
TRIGLIDAE, 511
Triodon bursarius, **1357**
Triple-tailed wrasse, **572**
Tripletails, 1265
Tripterodon, 1139
Tripterygion bapturum, **169**
Tripterygion etheostoma, **162, 473**
Trisotropis dermopterus, **1251**
Tri-spot wrasse, **440**
Tropidinus zonatus, **436**
Trumpetfishes, 773
Trunkfishes, 97
Trigonorrhina fasciata, **1396**
TRYPTERYGIIDAE, 636
Tunas, 1325
Turbot, 263
Turkeyfish, 258, **265, 512, 653**
Twinspot cardinalfish, **242**
Twinspot damselfish, **204**
Twinspot wrasse, **141, 575**

Two-banded anemonefish, **704**
Two-lined snapper, 222, **223**, **421**
Tylosurus giganteus, **332**
Tylosurus melanotus, **924**
Typee hawkfish, **488**

U

Undulate triggerfish, **119**, **124**
Unicorn leather-jacket, **125**
Unicorn razorfish, **132**
Unicornfish, **89**, **388**
Upeneus, 259, 739
Upeneus bensasi, **272**, **970**
Upeneus moluccensis, **971**, **972**
Upeneus tragula, **971**, **1463**, **1494**
Upeneus vittatus, **344**
URANOSCOPIDAE, 538
Uranoscopus bicinctus, **983**
Uranoscopus japonicus, **541**, **981**
Urolophus aurantiacus, **509**

V

Vagabond butterflyfish, **56**, **376**
Vanderhorstia ornatissimus, **475**
Variegated lizardfish, **338**
Variegated wrasse, **441**
Variola, 643
Variola louti, **490**, **1231**, **1492**
Velvetfishes, 641
Verasper variegatus, **1096**
Vermiculated angelfish, **36**, **37**
Vermiculated puffer, **409**
Vermiculated spinefoot, **389**
Violet-tinted soldierfish, **341**
Vireosa hanae, **475**

W

Wetmorella ocellata, **1580**
Wart-skin frogfish, **530**
Weevers, 467, 777
White-blotch moray eel, **354**
White-cheeked moray, **350**
White-faced surgeonfish, **91**
White-rim triggerfish, **120**
White-spotted boxfish, **101**
White-spotted tang, **88**
White-tailed damselfish, **202**
Whitings, **1003**
Wispy scorpionfish, **517**
Wobbegongs, 501, 1399
Wrasses, 128, 569, **1570**
Wrought-iron butterflyfish, **53**

X

Xanthichthys mento, **118**
Xanthichthys ringens, **1345**, **1627**
Xanthichthys sp., **1627**
Xiphasia matsubarai, **466**
(See *Xiphasia setifer*)
Xiphasia setifer, **466**
Xiphias gladius, **1258**
XIPHIIDAE, 1260
Xyrichthys taeniourus, **149**, **867**, **868**, **869**
(See *Hemipteronotus taeniourus*)

Y

Yellow-backed damselfish, **203**
Yellow-belly, **439**
Yellow conger eel, **352**
Yellow devil, **196**
Yellow-finned jack, **429**
Yellowfin goby, **179**
Yellow head angelfish, **35**
Yellow-lined sweetlips, **348**
Yellow-lined tripodfish, **392**
Yellow-mouthed moray, **353**
Yellow porgy, **438**
Yellow puffer, **403**
Yellow-streaked monocle-bream, **421**
Yellow-striped caesio, **223**
Yellow-striped snapper, **226**
Yellowtail, **427**, **428**
Yellow-tailed anemonefish, **180**, **185**
Yellow-tailed blenny, **469**
Yellow-tailed blue devil, **203**
Yellow-tailed cleaner, **447**
Yerutius, 219
Yongeichthys criniger, **1602**
Ypsiscarus ovifrons, **985**

Z

ZANCLIDAE, 75, 810
Zanclus, 75
Zanclus canescens, 75, **77**, **810**, **811**, **812**, **1156**, **1157**, **1605**
Zebra goby, **179**, **472**
Zebra lionfish, 265
Zebra moray, **354**
Zebra morwong, **247**
Zebra-striped Port Jackson shark, **506**
Zebrasoma, 797
Zebrasoma desjardinii, **84**, **799**
Zebrasoma flavescens, **84**, **385**, **1150**, **1151**
Zebrasoma scopas, **84**, **88**, **800**, **1150**, **1151**, **1152**, **1606**
Zebrasoma veliferum, **89**, **91**
Zebrasoma veliferum, **84**
(See *Zebrasoma desjardinii*)
Zebrasoma xanthurum, **384**, **798**
Zebrias zebra, **1100**
Zeus japonicus, **550**
Zigzag wrasse, **454**, **609**
Zoarchias veneficus, **161**
Zonogobius boreus, **178**